TIM ESTENSON'S
ON RAILS

ON RAILS

FROM ALCOHOLISM TO A MULTI-MILLION DOLLAR BRAND

TIM ESTENSON

&

DAVE FICERE

ON RAILS

Published by:
InTandem Digital Press
Text copyright © 2024 by Tim Estenson
First Edition
All rights reserved. No part of this book may be used or reproduced in any manner whatsoever without written permission except in the case of brief quotations embodied in critical articles and reviews. For more information on the book or to contact the authors, please visit onrailsbook.com
and contact onrailsbook@gmail.com.

Cover design by Lisa Lorbiecki at lisalorbiecki.myportfolio.com

All Photographs are the property of Tim Estenson
with the exception of "Christ Our Pilot"
©1950,1978 Warner Press, Inc., Anderson, Indiana.
Used with permission

ISBN-13: 978-1-7377374-9-0
Library of Congress Control Number: 2024919276

Publisher's Cataloging-in-Publication Data
Names: Estenson, Tim, author. | Ficere, Dave, author.
Title: On rails : from alcoholism to a multi-million dollar brand / by Tim Estenson & co-author Dave Ficere.
Description: Atlanta, GA: InTandem Digital Press, 2024.
Identifiers: LCCN: 2024919276 | ISBN: 978-1-7377374-8-3 (hardcover) | 978-1-7377374-9-0 (paperback) 978-1-7377374-7-6 (ebook)
Subjects: LCSH Estenson, Tim. | Businesspeople--Biography. | Motorcyclists--United States--Biography. | Motorcycle racing--United States. | Alcoholics--Biography. | BISAC BIOGRAPHY & AUTOBIOGRAPHY / Memoirs | BIOGRAPHY & AUTOBIOGRAPHY / Business | BIOGRAPHY & AUTOBIOGRAPHY / Sports | BUSINESS & ECONOMICS / Leadership | SELF-HELP / Substance Abuse & Addictions / General
Classification: LCC HC102.5 .E88 2024 | DDC 338.092--dc23

DEDICATIONS

This book is dedicated to my wonderful wife, Traci, and my children, Sami and Max. Your love, encouragement, and understanding have been my pillars of strength throughout this journey. We could not have completed this book without your unwavering support and belief in me.

Tim Estenson

To my wife, Patt, for her continued love, encouragement, helpful suggestions, and edits. This book would not have happened without you! Lotsa, Lotsa!

Dave Ficere

TABLE OF CONTENTS

Acknowledgements i
Foreword ii
Chapter 1: The Windowsill 1
Chapter 2: Lonely Beginnings 6
Chapter 3: Liquid Courage on the Badger Circuit 13
Chapter 4: The Apple Never Falls Far from the Tree 21
Chapter 5: Nearly Rock Bottom, But Not Yet 26
Chapter 6: A Not So Welcome Home 30
Chapter 7: Step One: Admit You Have A Problem 37
Chapter 8: St. John's 41
Chapter 9: Gino 47
Chapter 10: In Steel Beam We Trust 53
Chapter 11: White Outs 58
Chapter 12: Lost and Found 63
Chapter 13: Trying my Luck 67
Photographs 71-83
Chapter 14: Rolling the Dice 84
Chapter 15: Too Good to be True 89
Chapter 16: All on 23 Red 94
Chapter 17: Once in a Lifetime 101
Chapter 18: PT Boat or Aircraft Carrier? 107
Chapter 19: Fundamental Leadership Principles 115
Chapter 20: Know When to Hold 'Em & When to Fold 'Em . 119
Chapter 21: "Retirement". 126
Chapter 22: The Spiritual Journey 133
Chapter 23: Looking Back.. 138
Health and Wellness Resources 146
About the Authors 147

ACKNOWLEDGEMENTS

Thanks to my wife for introducing us and prompting me to tell my story and Dave for helping me write and edit it. For every one of my business associates and brothers in recovery, thank you for helping me with each step along my journey. Julia Maldonado, you have taught me much about writing and publishing a book, and I am grateful. To my teams at Estenson Logistics and Estenson Racing, you help me recapture my dream through your passion for racing. Thank you! My family has been with me every step of the way, and I wouldn't be where I am today without you!

Tim Estenson

I want to express my heartfelt gratitude to Catherine Anaya for introducing me to Tim, which marked the beginning of a wonderful friendship and this incredible journey. Tim (and Traci for prompting me), your trust in me to tell your story is a responsibility I deeply cherish. Julia Maldonado, your patience and guidance in refining the story has been invaluable. And to my beloved wife, Patt, your editing and writing suggestions have been a crucial part of this journey. We could not have done it without you!

Dave Ficere

FOREWORD

When I first met Tim it was through a mutual acquaintance, Jackie Mitchell. Jackie began a career in the car business after his time in flat track racing ended. I was a rep for Jackie early in my career and many years before knowing Tim. Jackie and I had a mutual passion and love of motorcycles, so I always looked forward to seeing him, doing some work together and then always talking about bike racing.

One day, Jackie called me and asked me if I knew who Tim Estenson was and would I be willing to meet with him. I told him of course I do, his flat track teams are the best and I knew if from the transportation industry as well. I have a personal rule I try to follow in my business life: Constantly seek out others who are more successful than you and develop a strong relationship with them. It doesn't matter the industry, just that they are successful. I do this to learn. Always learning and trying to better myself is a lifelong endeavor. It has helped me so much as I have grown my career in the car industry and developed relationships with successful executives, entrepreneurs and business owners. Tim Estenson certainly fit the bill and why I was eager to meet him.

When we met in Dallas a few weeks later, I was struck by how humble and warm Tim was. Most guys who reach the level of success that Tim has are not necessarily the kind of folks that make you comfortable the first time you meet them. And when you meet people like Tim you immediately want to hear their story and how they became successful.

As we sat at the table and just talked to one another I immediately felt at ease as we discussed his racing efforts and his business life. Tim never mentioned his early life and the struggles he had growing up. Why would he?

As I read an early draft of "On Rails" I was shocked. Shocked that Tim, one of the most successful people I know, dropped out of school in the 10th grade, was plagued by self-doubt and substance abuse and had overcome the odds against him to become the father, husband, successful business owner and servant of God he is today.

"On Rails" is deeply personal and inspiring. It is a raw and honest story of the challenges Tim faced throughout his life and how with the help of his faith, hard work, and family he overcame those challenges.

Andrew Gilleland
VP of Operations, Toyota Motor North America, Inc.

1

THE WINDOWSILL

Something is wrong, I realized as I woke up in my tiny cubby hole. My skin was crawling, and I had an overwhelming feeling of doom and dread. *Someone is coming to kill me*, I thought in panic. I stumbled to the apartment across the hall and asked Rick to give me something. "Mellow out," he said, seeing the panic in my eyes and hearing the fear in my voice.

Suddenly, and without warning, he was gone. *Strange*, I thought, because he never left his apartment. He even had his groceries delivered. Rick was a Vietnam veteran who had been hurt in the war, losing the use of his legs, although not the limbs themselves. As a result, he had a difficult time walking. I was shaking and sweating. *Oh shit, he's in on this*, I thought in my paranoia, figuring he was working with the people who were coming to get me. Frozen in fear, I could not control the shaking, so I found a beer in Rick's refrigerator, locked the front door behind me, and continued sweating uncontrollably. It never occurred to me to call 9-1-1 for help.

I stayed in the apartment waiting, opening and closing the blinds, and watching. I knew that at any moment, someone would break down the door and haul me off. It felt like an out-of-body experience. So, as I paced in the apartment, I began formulating a plan. *If someone breaks in, I'm not going to let them take me. I'll shoot myself in the head first.* I knew Rick had a pistol in the apartment because I had seen it once on the coffee table. I began looking around and found it in a dresser beside the bed. It was a revolver, already loaded, and I picked it up. I continued pacing around the apartment, swinging my arms in the air, waving the pistol around like a toy, just waiting for someone to come after me. I knew everything would end today, either by my own hand or someone else's. In my paranoia, I felt like there was a clamp on my head, realizing they would likely be coming in through the front door. So, I blocked it with a piece of furniture. *But wait. What if they decide to come through the window?* I asked myself.

I decided to sit on the windowsill, watching the street below for the people who were after me. Even though I was on the second floor, I made sure the windows were closed and locked. I began twirling the loaded pistol, finger on the trigger, as I sat at an angle in the two-foot-wide windowsill, back to the window, and waited; rocking back and forth while shaking uncontrollably.

My mind raced. *I can't do this anymore. I just need to kill myself.* My inner voice whispered as I put the gun to my head. I alternated between pointing the gun barrel at my temple and putting it in my mouth. Frozen by paranoia and keeping a firm grip on the gun, this went on for several hours. My paranoid delusion began at about 10:00 that morning. At some point, about six or seven hours later, I passed out, gun still in hand, finger on the trigger.

Wait, what was that noise? I awoke at about 9:00 p.m. to someone pounding on the barricaded front door. It was Rick. I was reluctant to let him back into his own apartment. Finally, I opened the door, the loaded gun in my hand, and pointed it at him. He did not get angry about me being in his apartment, but knew he had to talk me down.

"Tim, what are you doing? he simply asked. I've got some booze," he said, showing me the bottle in his hand. "Let's get fucked up together." He took the gun from me, put it away, and we began drinking the fifth of booze he had bought. "I know the feeling," Rick said when I finally let him in. "I know what you're going through.". He wasn't even pissed off that I was locked in his apartment and holding his gun. We drank the entire bottle, passed out, and woke up the next day in his apartment, totally hungover. The paranoia had disappeared, but I didn't know why. It was replaced by the shame of not even being able to kill myself.

"Damn, you better lighten up on the Moondust," Rick said.

Fuck, I'm not going to do Moondust anymore, I thought as I made my way back across the hall.

Apparently, Rick and I had smoked Moondust the night before. I was going through withdrawal when I climbed up onto the windowsill, gun in hand. He was my connection, and I would take whatever drugs he had. I remember he always had music playing in his apartment and spent his days watching television, drinking, and doing drugs. In the mid-1970s, a mixture of heroin and PCP known as "Moondust" was popular. Also known as "Angel Dust," when smoked in a bong or pipe, it caused unpredictable and wild behavior, including violence toward one's self or others. It can cause hallucinations, paranoia, and even psychosis. People taking it can feel detached from reality or their own consciousness. That sounded like me sitting on the windowsill the night before.

What should have been a wake-up call for me, I shrugged off as an "oh, well" moment and returned to my "apartment," which in and of itself was nothing more than a closet. Perhaps I should give you some background on what led to my windowsill moment.

My name is Tim Estenson, and I quit school in the tenth grade at 16 to pursue my passion for motorcycle racing, and to prevent being held back in school because of my poor grades. My other "passion" was alcohol. At this same time, I was already a full-blown alcoholic and drug user. After walking away from school, I followed my sister, Marcia, and her new husband to live in a small town in Iowa. *This is going to be my big racing breakout*, I thought, even though I had already experienced moderate success winning motorcycle races in North Dakota and throughout the Midwest.

I was so out of control that I remember staying up and drinking all night at the bachelor party, then going right from the party to the church. Totally drunk, I got dressed there and threw up right before the ceremony. In the middle of the wedding, I knew I was going to pass out, so I walked out of the church to the bathroom, threw up again, and then passed out from the drinking and lack of sleep. Despite it being her wedding day, my sister took it all in stride. "Well, that's Tim," she said. The reception was crazy, with people getting drunk and streaking, which was a fad then.

My sister let me sleep on the couch in their trailer and even got me a job at Mo's Motorcycle Shop, but I rarely showed up for work. While they were the responsible ones, I was a leech, living off of them and working only to make enough money to buy booze and drugs and get to my next race.

Eventually, Marcia got tired of my laziness and told me I had to move out. That is when I found my "apartment." In reality, it was a storage space under the stairwell of the apartment across the hall from Rick's that the tenants agreed to rent to me. It was a shit hole, so small that I couldn't even stand up. It was only for sleeping, but it didn't matter because I had no furniture, not even a mattress to sleep on. All I had was a sleeping bag and a bag of clothes. I didn't know anything different. I existed for the moment, day by day, never planning for tomorrow. I lived for just two things: Racing and getting high. One was the ultimate high where I felt good about myself, usually through a mixture of booze and drugs. You see, after spending most of the past two years constantly drinking, alcohol alone did not do it for me anymore. So, I started adding drugs to the mix. The equation was simple: The more I drank, the more I used. Marijuana and Speed were my drugs of choice, but eventually, I took whatever I could get from someone else for free. Which explains the Moondust.

The other important thing in my life was motorcycle racing. I loved racing and had already experienced some success. But slowly, the "ism" of alcoholism took over and surpassed the racing. I would live for the next drink, experiencing anxiety attacks (although I didn't know what they were) while waiting around all day for my evening binge to begin.

I mentioned Mo. Technically, I "worked" for him, but didn't do much. I would show up, putter around, and leave, making sure I made enough money to ride to the next race. In his own way, he was trying to help me. If any money was left, I would drink it away at the local popular bar, one of two in the small town. It was my "safe place," where they knew my name and a little bit about me, particularly my motorcycle riding. My typical routine was to drink until I either passed out or blacked out and somehow stumbled back to my eight-by-four storage space to sleep it off. Then, the next morning, I would wake up with remorse, fear, and overwhelming shame over the night before, even though I did not remember any of what had happened. There was not one single night I went to sleep sober. I just passed out and woke up in my closet. This was my routine, seven nights a week.

How could someone so young get so messed up, you ask? Well, let me go back to the beginning.

2

LONELY BEGINNINGS

My journey began on January 4, 1958, in my birthplace, Fargo, North Dakota. I lived there most of my life, sheltered from reality. We were a low-income family of five with my parents, my older brother, Mark, my sister, Marcia, and me. My mother was a stay-at-home mom, while my dad worked for the AT&T phone company.

As a small child, you don't know what you don't know, which was my experience. Although our family appeared "normal," from the outside, that was not the reality. We were dysfunctional, and all three of us kids were raised in that environment. My father was an active alcoholic and binge drinker, but ironically, there was never any alcohol in our home. Somehow, my mom kept it out of the house. There was always a silence surrounding my dad's drinking. As stoic Scandinavians, it was the elephant in the room that was never discussed. My sister, Marcia, shared her memories of our early childhood.

> When I started Kindergarten [that] was the first time I realized something was wrong. I hung onto what I thought was normal, which was hanging out with Tim.

Marcia, who is two years older, also remembered our dad being gone a lot, often returning with something special like a puppy or other gifts, trying to make up for his absence.

I felt like I had a pretty normal childhood, playing outside and sometimes being gone all day, only coming home for meals. One of the hobbies I enjoyed with friends was building forts and looking for stuff. We would hang out and play, but eventually, they would leave to spend time with or go someplace with their family. I had no such obligations, so I would end up by myself. Marcia had similar memories.

> There was not really any place to go, and I used to go to the skating rink. The owner would let us hang out there because there was nothing to go home to. He ended up being an excellent parental figure.

I do remember going to the skating rink, bringing a sandwich and staying from opening to closing. I also remember going to daycare at a young age and being scared, but I didn't know why. I was a fear-based person, afraid of the unknown. Being scared was my normal.

> "I shared the scared feelings, too," Marcia added. There was always a fear of what was coming next because of the ups and downs with our family. I don't remember anyone doing anything wrong to me, just the emotional, gut-wrenching fear.

I think that led to the feeling that something was off with both me personally and my family, even as a young child. But I did not know what or why. I think the feelings came from not understanding what was happening in our home. As a result, I never invited friends over, especially not to go inside our house. What I experienced was just a lot of loneliness, but I did not understand the feelings or their meaning. Marcia shared those feelings and also remembered never having friends over, either.

> My clothes weren't good enough, and the family was never good enough.

We really did not have a "normally functioning" family. We only had one car, which my dad drove, leaving my mom and us kids homebound. My dad worked different shifts, so he was home little, and apart from work, hung out at area bars. His behavior drove my mom's actions of hiding or covering up for him. My mom was on edge all the time because she did not know which "dad" would show up when he did come home. Would he be the happy drunk or the mean, angry drunk?

Trying to control everything inside the house and make it "perfect," was my mom's mode of operation. Keeping the house spotlessly clean was one thing she did to cope with the chaos my dad brought to the family. Even though my dad would not be home, she would cook dinner for us kids but not eat with us.. At a young age, I thought this was a "normal" life. *Everybody lives this way*, I thought. Marcia had similar feelings and shared her thoughts with me:

> For my mom, it was a big cover-up, trying to make things as normal as possible. We were ignored much of the time as she tried to cope with things. There was the hiding and denying of the disease, which had started when my dad was in the Navy. We did not have a clue what was going on (with our family). Tim felt normal to me; my older brother did not. We based our feelings on other families and what we saw in them.
>
> I remember our mom saying, "Messy on the inside, neat on the outside." That was our family mantra. We had to keep everything perfect on the outside because everything was so messed up on the inside." This must have been when we started having financial problems because about this time, my mom got a driver's license, a car, and went to work.
>
> We took care of each other. Tim and I hung out and looked out for each other, whereas my older brother lived in another world, taking care of things my dad should have been doing.

Tim also tended to get hurt a lot, one time getting smacked in the head by a spade while digging a hole. Another time, he got hit by a board in the attic. I also remember him being struck by a car while chasing a tricycle into the street.

I remember toward the end of the month when money was tight, the food combinations got really weird. I remember mom's creation she called 'mush.' Flour, milk, melted butter, and cinnamon mixed together. We also ate goulash, vegetables, noodles, and pasta. My mom got creative, fixing whatever food was available, even foods that did not go together. She made it work. *And creamed peas on toast,* I added. *Don't forget that. I hated it!*

As we grew up, we all coped with our home life in different ways, and despite not being close growing up, today, we are all very close emotionally. I would only do things I was good at and feared failing. That is where hockey came in. I cannot remember my parents coming to any hockey games, but Marcia came when she could. I think it was when I began Kindergarten that I started realizing something was different about my family. I remember coming home from school with questions, but did not know how to verbalize them since communicating feelings was frowned upon in our home. As I later went through counseling as an adult, I learned the history of dysfunctional behavior throughout my family. I remember hearing a statement that rang true to the point that I have never forgotten it:

> The average person is **raised** in a home;
> I simply **grew up** in a home.

Some of you know exactly what this means because you grew up like I did. My awakening that things were different came when I started school. I was so insecure and introverted that I really did not talk to anyone.

One of the things that I noticed was that most of my friends had a structured home life. They lived by rules, while I did not. I did not have the comprehension to understand why they had rules, and it confused me. Like, I don't remember ever sitting down with my parents to do homework with me. Things just weren't "typical" or "normal" for me. Sometimes, all my friends had to go home, but I had nowhere to go and would make up things to do to keep myself occupied. Marcia did something similar:

> I think this also was my world. But I had a long chore list and remember being dropped off at the grocery store with cash and a list. Even at a young age, I had to try figuring out how to cook food and prepare meals.

Later, we bought a house closer to the downtown area. I'm not sure why we moved, but the house had an upstairs bedroom, which we rented out to a single guy. While living there, I attended Jefferson Elementary School, where I finished Kindergarten. It was more fun. The teacher gave us assignments and provided some structure.

The only routine happened every Saturday night. We would see a movie at our house, our big treat for the week. We would watch the film and share a bowl of popcorn and a soda pop with the whole family. My dad may have sat in a few times, but it was mostly the rest of us trying to normalize something in our lives.

That felt nice and normal and a part of the structure I desperately wanted but did not know I was searching for. I began playing hockey in the third grade, lugging around an old army bag that held my second-hand gear. I would get up, go to school, come home, make a sandwich, put it in my hockey bag, and take it to the rink. Then, I would shoot the puck by myself, eat my sandwich, and stay entertained. Eventually, other kids showed up after doing their homework and eating dinner. I was always the first one there because I had nowhere else to go. I was a pretty good hockey player and made the fifth-grade team as a third-grader. This is where I felt like part of something, even though I did not feel worthy.

Playing hockey became an integral part of my life, but sadly, my parents never came to a game. In fact, one neighbor would take a group of us to our games in their old grain truck. I felt fortunate, because I had no other way to get around. During this time, I also began imitating some of my mom's controlling behavior. For example, I would take off my dirty clothes and fold them neatly into a pile. That was me trying to control something in my life.

Around seventh grade, my mom started working as a waitress as my dad's drinking worsened. Sometimes I would show up at her work, and she would feed me. I remember driving my bicycle there and getting a deep-fried grilled cheese sandwich called a "Cheese Frenchie."

Once, when I was in third grade, the school called my mom into the office. My dad may have also shown up, but I don't remember. The entire conversation centered around holding me back because of my mostly "D" grades. I threw a fit about being held back, and the school backed down. They did not realize that I did not have the tools to learn and was anxious about being called on in class. The only thing I had going for me was hockey, and if I got held back, it would have affected being able to play with my peers. That was my overriding concern.

When my dad was around, he began using me as an excuse to get out of the house. This began happening at a young age, even before I started elementary school. He would tell my mom he was going somewhere and taking me with him. She was delighted, thinking he was spending time with me. In reality, he would drive to a bar and leave me in the car for hours at a time. Another variation was he would take me with him, go to a friend's house, and leave me there while he and his buddy went to the bar. You can imagine how scared I was being left alone to sit in the car or with some people I didn't know. All I wanted to do was to go home. Marcia had a similar experience.

> Dad would drop me at the grocery store and pick me up an hour and a half later while he went to the bar.

I would be sitting by the window with what I had bought, waiting for him to show up.

I remember once Marcia and I decided to run away because we had had enough. I think I was in middle school, and Marcia was in high school. We packed our bags, walked to the Interstate, and hitchhiked to a friend's home in northern North Dakota, about two to three hours away. Our parents never looked for us, even though we were gone for a couple of weeks. Eventually, we just went home, and everyone acted like it never happened!

I also remember running away and hiding outside behind a tree, waiting for everyone to go to bed, and then going back into the house. Another time, I was out with my BB gun, and my mom was at the kitchen sink. She turned and started walking toward me. "Don't take another step, or I'll shoot," I said. She did; I shot and put a hole in the window, just missing her head. Marcia summed up our childhood best:

> We both had to find a reason for survival and to wake up the next day. We knew we had to survive for the other person.

Marcia and I came to the same conclusion. We never had the opportunity to just be kids. The same could be said for my older brother, Mark, who recently visited me. As we discussed this book, he began sharing some of his memories. He started working at the age of 12, and my mom made him the man of the house while he was still in high school. He told me she controlled his every move, even his social life. Once, he came home with a girl, and they were relaxing out in the neighbor's yard. Our mom came out and berated him for lying around. "We've got things to do," she said. When he answered her back, she smacked him in the head. By the age of 14, Mark was working ten hours a day every Saturday and Sunday as a mechanic, in addition to working during the week. Despite working hard and getting good grades he could not graduate high school because he did not attend gym class.

3

LIQUID COURAGE ON THE BADGER CIRCUIT

My life changed forever the day I had my first drink. In the seventh or eighth grade, I was hanging out with friends by the lake, where we spent our summers. I remember walking into the woods with a group of people. Someone in the group had some of the little booze bottles you get on an airplane, and we began drinking them. One particular drink was Everclear, the strongest drink on the market. Ironically, because of my dad's drinking, I had sworn not to become like him. I was afraid to drink and dumped the first one out after pretending to drink it.

However, peer pressure got to me, and I took that first drink. That and subsequent drinks immediately removed my feelings of inferiority. It gave me courage and confidence and made me feel "a part of" something. It filled in everything I felt had been missing from my life. As I did with most things in life, I jumped all in. My first drink ended up with me getting stone drunk, blacking out, and eventually passing out. My sister, Marcia, came to the rescue, as she often did, although I don't remember anything about it. She later told me:

> One of the kids let me know where you were because you were passed out." The first thing I figured out was how to get you home. I think someone had a car, so I was able to get their help. Emotionally, I was

> surprised, disappointed, scared, and mad at you for being so out of it. After I got you back home, I don't remember what happened. I just had to figure out how to make you okay.

Because I was desperately searching for something, I did not become a social drinker when I discovered alcohol. I instantly became an alcoholic. Every time I drank, it was for feeling and effect. I immediately went from zero to 100.

I was never a throw-up drinker but a blackout drinker. I would black out for 30 minutes or so, wake up, and black out again, losing two to three hours in the process. I remember driving home when I was 16, getting about three blocks away, and the next thing I knew, I was somewhere else. I had driven past our house and could not find our driveway. This happened more than ten times, and it is a miracle I wasn't killed or did not hurt someone else.

My life changed significantly that summer at the lake. I began drinking regularly and discovered the feelings I had always searched for. For me, the fine line between the normalcy of being a social drinker and getting drunk did not exist. I did not know what it meant to be a "social drinker." For me, I would only stop drinking when we ran out of booze. Had I not had Marcia to take care of me, I don't know where I would be today. I was that far gone and out of control. Marcia had a different experience.

> While I was going through some of the same things, it was different because I was older. I was in high school and working, so I had other priorities. I do remember that Tim could have played varsity hockey as a freshman, but his drinking got in the way.

I had played [hockey]in school and on travel (club) teams, but no one wanted to play us because we were so good. I did not even realize I was that good at hockey because of my poor self-esteem. I felt inadequate, even though I was a good hockey player.

Part of my problem, in addition to the drinking, was my attitude. I remember getting called into the coach's office and being told about his and the team's expectations. They actually expected me to show up to practice! I took offense to that, and somehow felt above following his rules. I felt entitled to do what I wanted to do. My belligerent attitude was, "No one is going to tell me what to do." This continued for a while, but I never got kicked off the team. I just stopped showing up. My priorities were messed up, and I was often described as someone who does not detach but amputates. I would just cut things or people out of my life if they didn't fit into my view of how things should be. When sober, I was an introvert who did not talk to people except friends. Alcohol became my crutch. It gave me boldness and an attitude that was the exact opposite of my sober self.

My middle school years were turbulent as well. As I mentioned earlier, I discovered smoking in the seventh grade and alcohol shortly after that. By the ninth grade, I had identified what drinking did for me. Alcohol magnified my feelings, mostly those of depression, anger, happiness, and sadness. During ninth and tenth grade, life was spiraling out of control. I discovered I could be anything I wanted to be when I was drinking. In my mind, I suddenly "fit in" and was as good as anyone else. I went from feeling inferior to feeling equal or even superior. This marked the beginning of my substance abuse cycle, but I didn't see that I was becoming like my dad. Ironically, I kept saying, "I'll never be like my dad," but I was well on that path. Ironically enough, this was the same time that my dad went to the impatient treatment center and my mom found help at Al-Anon."

While in high school, I remember sitting back and looking at the different groups and seeing that I didn't fit in anywhere, among the jocks, stoners, or geeks. As a result, I would never go into the lunchroom because there were no groups I could sit with. Most of the time, I ended up eating my lunch by myself. At this point, my life revolved around drinking and finding others to party with. Because alcoholism is progressive, I kept going downhill, but I was still racing and winning, despite my downward spiral. But if I wasn't racing, everything was about looking for the next drink.

As is the case with most addicts, I started hanging out with other drinkers, and my behavior became worse. I pushed anybody in my life away who cared about me or did not drink as I did. I could not be around them because I knew they would see how bad I was. I would go into a shell to protect myself, leeching onto others who were like me. My parents tried to help me by pushing me through school, but I got kicked out of Fargo South High School in the tenth grade. I also got expelled from a second and third school and even a GED school.

Besides alcohol, my passion was motorcycle racing, which started when I was 10 or 11. But I waited until I was 15 to get my novice license. I was racing motorcycles at that time and winning races. When I won, people would go crazy, but I didn't understand the big deal. All I was looking forward to was the payout so I could buy gas and beer. Drinking made me a different person, giving me the boldness I did not have when I was sober. The alcohol was an artificial fix for my incredibly low self-esteem. Still, I sheltered myself, and so few people saw my inward changes. Even at school, I never thought girls liked or would want to date me, so I never put myself out there. My fears kept me from engaging with the opposite sex. But girls noticed me at races, hanging around, enamored by and following me, but I never saw them. Marcia remembered them hanging around and me not noticing them. She actually called them "groupies." She said I was too busy racing to notice.

One night at Glyndon Speedway, I entered several races and won every one, even when forced to start from the back row, but I was easily pissed off if things didn't go my way. Once, I lost my chain and pushed the motorcycle down, striking Marcia. I felt terrible. Besides hockey, racing was my only affirmation. For me, the adrenaline from racing replaced the high from alcohol, and I tried to match that rush. I always sought to do my best on the track and finish in a good spot. If I lost, it wrecked my self-esteem.

My racing journey started at the local level. You would have to earn so many points on this "Badger Circuit" to become an American Motorcyclist Association (AMA) Novice. There were so many people racing motorcycles that sometimes as many as 200 riders showed up, so you would have to enter qualifying races to try for one of the

16 spots in the feature race. I did really well and earned my novice license exceptionally fast. While most people took two years, I did it in about six months. I wasn't even old enough to race legally, so my dad had to sign a waiver for me to complete it. My journey from novice racing to getting onto the AMA circuit was more than just eye-opening. This was me leaving everything I knew and the small town areas I was familiar with. I remember traveling to Daytona, Florida, the first time I ventured outside the Midwest to race. We stopped in Atlanta, Georgia, and had to go downtown for something. We found a local bar, which was the first time I encountered minority people in large numbers. As the only Caucasians in the bar, I was scared to death. That just wasn't part of my world in nearly all-white North Dakota. Shocking today, yes, but remember fear was my norm and I didn't know anything different.

A group of us, including Marcia and her then-boyfriend, traveled around the race circuit. He was also a racer, while she worked for the Badger Circuit. The racing was still the most important thing to me, but the alcohol was just as significant. One of the most important things we did before pulling into the pits was to get the ice and beer for the post-race celebration. Hopefully, among all the riders, we had won some money. Despite my success, sponsorship was not widespread, so finances were always tight.

I never drank before a race. However, when the race was over, I would start drinking recklessly, and we would hit the road. We would stop and get gas, often filling up and not paying for all of it, back in the day when you would fill up first, then pay. We would stop at county fairs and race for money, hoping to make enough to get to the next race. In a typical year, that describes our life. I would drink myself from one race to another. Marcia remembers those days:

> Typically, we had to drive all night long to get to the next race location. We were racing two to three times a week, so there were always long drives to get to the next location.

We would not have much money for food. If we had breakfast at a restaurant, there were times we would skip out on the bill. One place described me as 'the strawberry pancake' girl after we took off without paying and had to come up with the cash to settle up. Fortunately, no one called the cops on us. I never questioned this lifestyle because this was just the way we lived. But once we got out of it, we realized how crazy our lives had been. But we were young, and it seemed normal to us at the time.

We went through a period when friends of ours started getting killed racing. One summer, we lost at least three of our friends. I remember things going wrong, like getting caught stealing gas or food and the deaths of fellow riders.

I thought we were doing all this so Tim could become an AMA racer. There was a group of people doing what we were doing, but some of them had financial backing, so they may not have been as broke as we were.

We would carpool in vans to the next place. Everyone in our group was friendly until we hit the racetrack, and then we became competitive and not cordial. After the race, we would drink together and become friends again. I remember my alcohol use increased as we lost friends, who were killed. Or we would smoke a lot of dope. One guy invented a motorcycle-looking bong that we used as well. The partying got worse and worse for me in between races as we traveled around. I think it was my way of dealing with the losses all around me.

A few times during the winter, we could afford a Best Western motel and would have as many as eight people in a room. Once we got so drunk, we started throwing furniture off the balcony into the frozen pool, as a rock star might do. Still, I had no concept of reality, and I would fight any sense of authority, being a real asshole in the process. But through it all, and even with the deaths and accidents of other riders, I don't think I ever had a motorcycle accident or broke any bones. I overcompensated, riding harder because I did not have the best equipment. Still, I remember once dropping off a friend at the local hospital after he overdosed. Not wanting to get caught with drugs or alcohol, we left him there, where I heard he nearly died. Thankfully, he recovered from that ordeal.

4

THE APPLE NEVER FALLS FAR FROM THE TREE

One of my life's most significant transitions happened between the eighth and ninth grades. My dad worked long hours, hit the bars after work, and was not involved in the family. This was the period in my life when alcoholism started taking over, even though I was still focused on my racing. Sadly, I chose my destructive lifestyle over hockey during this time as well and began living for the "next moment."

My dad, Morris Jr. (Morrie), worked nights or swing shifts at AT&T's main building in downtown Fargo. He had moved up through the company, starting as a pole climber, becoming an installer, and eventually a manager. At this point in my life, his job included monitoring the electronics and cabling for special events, such as a World Wrestling Federation match. In this capacity, he would sit inside the building, supervising the electronics, ensuring everything went well and that all systems functioned as designed. In typical male, or perhaps Scandinavian fashion, he did not talk about his work. It became another thing in our family that was not discussed.

My dad's lack of family involvement was not just confined to the work week. On a typical weekend, he would watch television and smoke cigarettes. Pall Mall straights, as I remember. Occasionally, he would load us into the car and drive to Ada, Minnesota, where he was born. For some reason, I always got car sick on these trips to visit his parents and my grandparents. These visits added to our family drama. We would stay with my dad's parents, where I saw more dysfunctional living. My grandfather, Morris Sr., was a drinker and controlling. At the same time, my grandmother, Bennie, was heavily addicted to prescription drugs, which my grandfather suppplied her with. Even though we were kids, we would just sit there. This is at a time when kids were supposed to be seen and not heard and spend their time playing. Our only outlet was a nearby park, where we could play horseshoes and use the playground equipment, like the swing set and teeter-totter. My sister reminded me that we didn't see our grandparents very often because (we think) they were afraid we would figure out the family's secrets.

Things weren't much better when we visited my mother's parents, who also lived in Ada. My mom, LaVonne, who went by the nickname Bonnie, was the youngest of 11 children in a farming family. She was the "surprise" and unwanted child who was given away to one of the aunts and passed around to other relatives her entire life. Growing up this way became part of the abandonment issues she battled throughout her life.

When we visited their house, my grandfather would sit in his rocking chair in their tiny living room with the TV and a spittoon. He could hit that spittoon every time, even from great distances, and I was enamored by that. Watching him hit that spittoon was like a work of art. Otherwise, these stays were very uncomfortable for the entire family. They were always kept short, so short that I don't remember ever eating a meal there. The visits were a family ritual, done out of duty, not out of joy or pleasure. Even though we went often, I never felt like I really knew them. In the last few years of my grandmother's life, my mom tried to nurture the relationship with her mom after my grandfather died. This process began after my mom got into Al-Anon.

I mentioned that my dad's mom was addicted to prescription drugs. She eventually died from a drug overdose, and there is still conjecture within my family whether it was accidental or not. After she died, my grandfather on my dad's side was left on his own and increased his drinking. He would guilt my dad into visiting him, but those visits were short and without purpose. Grandpa eventually died from alcoholism. I learned from my recovery work that many people in my family rewrote history and that I had to learn to find out the real truth about the people and events that shaped me.

The more I was around other people who seemed to know how to cope with their own emotions, the more I realized something was wrong. I knew I did not have the tools to deal with these issues. I did not feel I was as good as other people because I kept secrets and did not know how to deal with either their issues or my own. As a result, I began lying about everything, even if I would be better off telling the truth. It wasn't long before my lies became my reality. Living in that false reality, I was trying to be something I wasn't. It was like a suit of armor, a shield against people hurting me. I was not letting anyone close and was utilizing a protection mechanism without knowing it. I knew I did not feel as good as the people around me. I subconsciously compared my insides to other people's outsides, which is a common trait among addicts. Alcohol was my way of coping, trying to maintain a high where I felt "normal." Alcohol also made me feel better than other people.

I started realizing how I was coping when I began attending Alateen meetings, where I saw how my dad was and how that affected me. Unfortunately, those facilitating the meetings were coming too close to discovering me, which made me angry and caused me to flee.

Someone asked me if my parents reinforced these feelings of self-doubt in me. The simple answer is no, at least directly, because they mostly ignored me. In ninth grade, my mom went to her Al-Anon meetings, but she would tell me to be home at a specific time. I just laughed and defiantly replied, "I'll be home when I want," and left. When I returned, she would give me the third degree about where I had been and what I had been doing. I simply lied to her about my drinking. Even when I brought my buddy Peter home with me because he was too drunk to go home, my mom would be totally oblivious to our falling-down-drunk behavior. Years later, in my recovery work, I learned that living in denial was her "go-to," as was sweeping things under the rug.

As an adolescent, I was unprepared for everything in life: work, sex, growing up, and dealing with changing emotions. My behaviors were out of control, and I was the kid who did crazy things, dared others, or accepted their dares. For example, one winter, my buddies thought jumping over a house with our snowmobile was possible because the snowbanks had built up around the house. The idea was to run up the snowbank, land on the roof, and clear the house. The problem was no one wanted to try it, so I did. The snowbank collapsed as I hit it, and I smashed the brand-new snowmobile (which we did not own) into the house, breaking the handlebars, windshield, and skis. I escaped with some bumps, bruises, and black and blue marks but didn't break anything. The behavior was my attempt to get noticed and accepted, almost like someone jumping up and down, waving their arms, and shouting, "Notice me!" By the way, my dad came outside when he heard the noise, shook his head, and went back inside. He didn't say a word.

As alcoholism became a part of my life, it continued a familiar pattern in my family. I think my dad's alcoholism stemmed in part from his upbringing. Let's be clear: my dad's alcoholism was not his parent's fault, but their influence was definitely a factor in his upbringing and subsequent addiction. And that impacted me and my addiction, as well. Alcohol is cunning, baffling, and addictive, and Obsessive Compulsive Disorder (OCD) is definitely a factor in the disease. Eventually, the OCD component and the lack of control took over. My grandfather was an alcoholic, so it's not hard to understand why my dad and I eventually went down that road.

I don't remember how old I was when my dad began getting help for his alcoholism. I may have been in ninth grade because we had to attend "family meetings" at The Heartview Alcoholism Treatment Clinic. Marcia remembers my 'issues' being discovered fairly quickly during these meetings, particularly at this Bismarck facility that dealt with alcohol and drug addiction issues.

My memories of those meetings are vague, and I don't recall how I reacted to the counselors calling me out on my stuff. I remember my mom had gotten into Al-Anon maybe six months before my dad went into treatment. At Heartview, Dad got clean and sober and started trying to work through the wreckage of his past. Because we had no money, he also got a second job at night to pay off our debts.

I was forced to Alateen meetings for children of alcoholics and remember driving to them, so I must have been about 16. I remember a recovering alcoholic coming to talk to the group and answer questions. I wouldn't speak to him, but he pulled me aside.

"I look forward to seeing you in AA in the future," he said, looking me dead in the eye. Without knowing it, he was speaking prophetically.

"I am an alcoholic, and I'm going to run this as far as I can," I remember saying to myself at the age of 16. *When I hit the end, I'll get help*, I thought. I took this attitude so far that I would try to recruit others to participate in my addictive behavior.

In my mind, everyone was "after me," and I needed to get out of there. My dad had gotten sober and turned his life around, so I was now the screwed-up standout in my family. Suddenly, it's "all eyes on Tim," and Alateen made me see who I really was. While I attended for a while, instead of asking for help, I was fully committed to being an alcoholic.

Despite my condition, I knew that if I ever decided I wanted help, all I had to do was ask my parents, because they seemed to have figured out their issues. Once, they even did a formal intervention for me, which I just walked out of in anger. Becoming my dad made me spiral downward further into my addiction.

The common denominator, also known as the "ism" in alcoholism, is trying to fill the void of something lacking in our lives. Whether one is talking about overeating, sex, alcohol, or any other addiction, it seeks to fill that void that only God can fill. The sad truth about alcoholism is that as it takes over, the shame kicks in, and you drink to try to suppress the shame. It becomes a vicious and endless cycle.

5

NEARLY ROCK BOTTOM, BUT NOT YET

After the windowsill moment and Moondust high I mentioned in Chapter 1, I immediately went back to my regular partying routine. That's right, no lesson learned. I wanted to go someplace else but had no way to get there. So, a friend and I found a car with the keys left in it, "borrowed" it, and went to Sioux City, Iowa. We tried to get into a strip club, but the bouncer would not let me in because my fake ID was totally inaccurate. I was about 5'8 or 5'9 and weighed 120 pounds, but the ID described me as 6'2, 220, with red hair. Not even close! I was already stumbling drunk, and the bouncer didn't appreciate my abusive behavior. "You gotta get out of here before I call the cops," he told me. So, I had to walk back and sit in the stolen car while my racing buddies, including my friend Larry, spent time inside the club. As a footnote, we beat the crap out of the stolen car and drove it out in the country and burnt it up.

At the time, my sister's husband was not a stellar guy. Because of that, Marcia started hanging out more with a friend of mine, Mike, eventually leaving her husband and dating Mike. They drove to Peoria, Illinois, where Mike lived with his grandmother and worked in a motorcycle shop. Naturally, I tagged along with the idea of continuing my racing there. I drove my car, a four-door Dodge Coronet that I named Clarence and brought a motorcycle. I tore out the car's back seat and put my bike in the vacated space. I went from city to city to race, continuing my crazy lifestyle. I always slept in Mike's burnt orange Dodge van and rarely got a hotel room. This was a dark time for me because I was totally disconnected from anyone in Fargo and alone most of the time.

I remember once being at a bar in Trivoli, Illinois, when I got a call. Mike had stolen a brand-new van because his orange one was on its last legs. So, we began switching everything from the old van, including the license plate, making me an accomplice to a crime. Meanwhile, we continued to race and make money, repeating our same destructive pattern. Mike and Marcia worked it out to get me a room in Trivoli, which was within walking distance of the bar. I was there for a few months, and during the day, I just walked around, having nowhere to go and not knowing what to do because everyone else had a life, and I didn't. My body and mind were messed up, and I knew it but could not identify what was wrong. My daily goal was to make enough money to drink that night. I was experiencing the windowsill feelings again, but this time without the withdrawals. I was good at playing the game and making things look right from the outside, but inside I was a mess. I also felt a lot of pressure racing, knowing I had to win enough money to survive and continue my lifestyle.

One night, I was back at Marcia and Mike's apartment, and we decided to go to the local bar where I spent most of my time. I drank so much that my sister and Mike left, sick and tired of me and my antics. I drank myself into a blackout and woke up outside the bar in front of a police car with lights flashing. The next thing I knew, they were throwing me up against the car. I got away, started running, blacked out again, and woke up with my hands cuffed behind me.

I woke up on a Saturday morning in a cell at the run-down Peoria County jail, which I later learned had been condemned. I had no idea what I had done. Had I killed someone? Was I just drunk and belligerent? I did not have a clue, as the previous night was a blur. Later, I found out I kicked the cop in the nuts as I fell into the car's backseat before blacking out again.

I also realized I was supposed to be leaving to go race that afternoon. Instead, I was facing multiple charges, including resisting arrest and running away from the cops. After my initial appearance

before a judge and hearing the charges at what they called "short court," I returned to the cell, thinking, "Oh, my God, that is not me!"

As I usually did when I was in trouble, I called my sister. Soon, through the tiny cell window, I saw Marcia and Mike arrive in the burnt orange van. I watched my sister get out and walk across the street toward the jail. I was so happy because I would soon be free. Suddenly, I saw her leave, return to the van, and drive away. Later, I found out they couldn't afford the bond and had to go to get to the race I was supposed to attend. Complicating matters was the fact that it was a three-day weekend, so it would be Tuesday before I could be freed.

While I was out of my cell, making my phone call, some of the other inmates stole my mattress, pillow, and other stuff. They wanted to kill me, but I was locked in, so they couldn't get to me. I got through the long weekend, scared to death, and couldn't wait to get out of there. When Tuesday arrived, the judge read the charges and said I could get out on bail. The only problem was I had no bail money.

"Young man, where is your attorney?" the judge asked.

"Your honor, I did not know I would need an attorney, and I have no idea why I am here, except I know I drank too much," was my clueless reply. I had thrown some chairs and other stuff in the bar, which is why I got kicked out, and the cops were called. But of course, I didn't remember any of it.

"Can anyone bail you out?"

"No," I said, "I don't have anyone other than my sister, but she does not have enough money," I replied.

The authorities returned me to my cell and later decided to lower my bond, get me an attorney, and have me pay the fines. Finally, the judge called me back in and said it was my "lucky day" because the officer I assaulted decided to drop the charges. The authorities agreed to release me but demanded I leave Illinois immediately and never come back.

"I'm sorry, I can't do that because I don't have gas money to get out of town," I told them, knowing I still needed to get my car out of impound. Wanting to get rid of me, the judge gave me my car back, and my sister returned with enough gas money to get me out of town. Somehow, my parents had sent her the funds for me to return home to Fargo.

6

A NOT SO WELCOME HOME

Most mapping applications say the nearly 700-mile journey from Peoria, Illinois, to Fargo, North Dakota, should take about ten hours. Mine took six days. I refer to this trek as my "trip of shame" because that is precisely what it was. I had nothing except my car, motorcycle (stuffed inside the car), and the clothes on my back. Everything else was gone. My sister had succeeded in getting me out of town and was glad to see me go because now I would be someone else's problem, not hers. The shame within me was real. I felt I had hit rock bottom physically, emotionally, and mentally. Deep inside, I knew I had to return home because I had nowhere else to go. So, I drove straight through, only stopping for gas.

The closer I got, the more I felt I would be okay. Especially as I started reaching my "safety zone," the geographical area a few hundred miles from Fargo/Moorhead. In reality, my thinking process was distorted under the alcoholic brain that overpowered everything else. I was totally deceiving myself, thinking I would be welcomed back with open arms, even though I had burned most of my bridges. As I got closer, my alcoholic brain continued deceiving me, saying *this time would be different.*

There was something different. My family had it with me, and I was apprehensive about how I would be received when I showed up on my parent's doorstep. I was in a quandary, not knowing what to do. The "right thing" was to go home, but I didn't want to return there, even though my parents were expecting me to show up, as my sister had told them I was coming home. But I didn't care about their expectations. I decided I wouldn't go straight home but divert to the home of one of the few friends I had left. I must admit that much of what happened next was and still is a blur. Before heading to my friend's house, I exited the freeway and went to a bar where I knew they would serve me. The place was empty, as it was early afternoon, and I had a sinking feeling in my stomach, full of remorse, loss, and despair.

All I wanted to do was order a beer and nurse it until other people showed up and started buying me drinks. I was so desperate that if patrons left some beer in their glass after leaving the bar, I would quickly go over to their table and drink it. The same goes for cigarettes. I would smoke the leftover butts in the ashtray. That is how low I had sunk. As I said, I had nothing. My despair was real, but it was a different feeling than I had ever had. I felt that I had let everybody down, including my family. I could not even boast about my racing career. I was such a mess and so skinny at 5'9" and 120 pounds that I looked sickly. It didn't help that I hardly ever ate. When I awoke each day, my goal was to find a way to drink that night.

Meanwhile, back at the bar, my thinking was so messed up that I knew I had to "work" people to get them to buy me a drink. After being at the bar since about 2:00 p.m., the crowd began showing up as evening began, so I stayed, enjoying the live band while smoking and drinking with people I didn't even know. I got totally wasted that night, ending up passed out at some guy's house. Of course, it was someone I didn't even know. The next day, I woke up and managed to stay drunk and stoned for the next two days, again leeching off others I had met until they kicked me out. I had forgotten about all the devastation, thinking I was safe and okay because I was back in my hometown.

Somehow, on the second day, I ended up in a Ford Econoline van. I had gotten stoned with the people I was with. On the second day they drove me to my parents' house in their van. I remember being so out of it that at one point, the big side door of the van was open, and I was spread out, my head on the step. Sprawled out on a sea of empty beer cans and reeking of pot smoke, I looked up. My father was looking down at me. He shook his head, slammed the door closed, and went back inside the house. That was my "triumphant" welcome home.

Later, I exited the van and walked inside the house through the side door, hoping my mom wasn't in the kitchen. I went down the steep stairs to a sleeping area with a concrete floor and walls and went to sleep or passed out. I'm not sure which. This marked the beginning of my addiction spiraling out of control and them trying to help me. I would get a job, consistently show up late, get fired, and find another job. I could fix anything and eventually got hired as a welder for Steiger Tractor. I worked from 3:00 to 11:00 p.m., which was perfect. The hours allowed me to sleep late, work, get off in time to hit the bars and party, go home, and sleep it off. I moved in with a couple of guys from Steiger, and we followed the same routine of drinking, smoking dope, and then going to work. It was a vicious cycle, but it gave me the money to fund my lifestyle. Eventually, I stopped showing up at Steiger and got fired. At that point, my parents told me I wasn't welcome in their home until I got help.

My pattern was so repetitive that it almost does not bear repeating. For me, every day was like the movie "Groundhog Day." I would wake up, and the remorse would hit. Every morning, the big question was how to get enough money to start getting drunk. But drinking was becoming less effective in numbing my pain. Not knowing how to find the maximum or "perfect" high, I would drink so much that I would "drink myself sober."

The pattern typically started with drinking to the point of being happy and having fun, then suddenly becoming unbalanced and slobbering. I would get to the point where I couldn't remember how I got someplace, and suddenly, my head would clear. This is how I defined drinking myself sober, and I was totally aware that I was doing so. My senses and clarity would return. My solution was to drink even more or think about killing myself, although I did not have the courage to do it. During this period of my addiction, I always had a bottle of Mad Dog 20/20 under my car seat. I would pull it out and drink it by myself.

Part of hitting rock bottom included alienating my friends and pushing them away. It was a gradual process, some of which happened while I was racing. It was hard to keep in touch with people since there was no social media or cell phones. Also, because of my racing success, I projected an "I'm better than everyone else" attitude, which put off many people. Once I returned home after my prolonged absence, some friends were willing to give me a second chance, but others saw I was now worse than ever. They, like most of my family members, were soon done with me, too.

A couple of people did hang around. When I was working swing shifts at Steiger, I met Marty. He was from a little town in South Dakota, lived in a trailer with several people, and we became drinking buddies. I also had one friend, Larry, from my racing days. He stuck around and tried to help me, but eventually, I alienated Larry and Marty, too.

Larry's parents let me move into their house, and one Thursday, he drove to Fargo in his van and told me we were going to party all weekend. We began drinking at various house parties and bars as soon as he arrived. We picked up Marty, and all ended up at a party, where we met some girls. Marty had heard about a big kegger party on Saturday, so all of us piled into the van and started heading south on I-29, smoking pot and drinking beer along the way. Since I was the "most sober" of the group, I was driving. Suddenly, I saw flashing lights in my rearview mirror. We were being pulled over by the police.

As the officer approached the van, I had the bright idea of having the guys toss the empty cans out the side doors into the ditch as I rolled down the window. The van reeked of marijuana smoke and beer.

"Do you know why I pulled you over?" the Highway Patrol officer asked.

I didn't.

He said I was driving too slowly on the Interstate. He had clocked me at only 35 miles per hour. Suspicious enough to get his attention.

"Whose van is this?" he asked.

"Larry's," I replied, "but he is too drunk to drive."

"Have you been drinking?"

"Yes, but not enough to bother me," I quickly replied.

The officer could have run us all in, as we were all under 18 except for Larry. Instead, he just told me to go home. We ignored that advice and continued looking for the kegger party. There was no way we should have been let go, but that was my story. I was always escaping much-deserved consequences for my bad behavior.

Sometime later, we were driving on some side streets, trying to find the party, when I got pulled over again, this time by a city police officer. Because I had started drinking again after being pulled over the first time, by now, I was completely drunk and slurring my words. Amazingly, the officer wanted to let us go.

"Just let the other guy drive, I'll follow you, and you park the vehicle," he told me, apparently not wanting to deal with any of us.

"Officer, I can't do that, these people are too drunk to drive, but I'm fine," I told him. Again, we escaped being arrested, and I suffered no consequences for my reckless behavior.

After a short sleep break at someone's house, we returned to the van and drove south on I-29. The girls said they had to go home because, by now, it was 3:00 a.m. Saturday morning. But we didn't take them home. Instead, I drove to Sisseton, South Dakota, and parked the van in the center of the city park. On the grass in the middle of the town square. I passed out, and no one could wake me up. Finally, I came to in the early afternoon, and the girls kept saying they had to go home. But we were in Marty's hometown and going to the kegger that night. Someone came to pick up the girls, and suddenly, they were gone. It was just Larry, Marty, and me, drinking in his hometown bar, "warming up" for that night's kegger party.

Even though I was a small guy, I would pick fights with people bigger than me when I got drunk. I think it was part of my "death wish," hoping someone would beat me to a pulp and put me out of my misery. Well, in the bar, some big farmer-type young guys were playing pool, and I set my quarter on the table's edge, indicating I had the next game. Marty knew these guys (remember, this is his hometown), but they didn't like this long-haired, skinny freak interrupting their game. The next thing I remember is walking over and hitting one of the big guys with a pool cue, and he responded by beating the crap out of me. Cooler heads prevailed when Harold, one of Marty's friends, intervened and talked the big guys out of hurting me.

Harold and Marty realized they had to get me out of there for my own good. So, we left and went to Harold's parents' house to sober up and regroup before heading out to the party in Larry's van. Shortly after arriving, Harold and Marty left, fed up with my antics, leaving Larry and me alone at this farm kegger party. We smoked dope and drank all night, but soon Larry and I started arguing. He wanted to leave since we didn't know anyone there, but I hated to give up on a good party. We got into a fistfight outside. "Screw this," Larry said. I went back inside as my last friend drove off without me.

Everything was fuzzy after that. I remember waking up lying in the farmhouse hallway, not knowing where I was, who lived there, or how I even got there.

I can't do this anymore, I thought, remembering what my mom said when she told me I was no longer welcome in their home.

"If you ever reach the point where you can't do this anymore, we're here for you and will help you," she said in tough love after she and my dad got into recovery for their own issues.

Someone gave me a ride back to Fargo, nearly 100 miles away, and I crept into my parent's house through the side door and went down to the basement. I lay down in the bed in the fetal position, paralyzed, not knowing what to do anymore. When my mom showed up, I was stone-faced, realizing I couldn't keep killing myself. I had gone all-in, 100% in my addiction, and knew I was either going to die or get help. It was September 19, 1976, when I realized I couldn't live this way anymore. Finally, I had hit rock bottom after the three-day weekend binge of my lengthy alcohol addiction. My life was about to change dramatically.

7

STEP ONE: ADMIT YOU HAVE A PROBLEM

I holed up in the basement but did nothing. I remember sitting on the side of my bed, realizing I needed help. But I felt only desperation for the next few days after returning home. I had nothing and was coming off a couple of years of self-abuse with drugs, alcohol, and not eating. I was just numb and spent time staring into space, not knowing what to do next. There were times I just laid in my basement bed, frozen, saying, "I'm going to get up now," but unable to do so. It was like watching someone else's life in an out-of-body experience. I realized I had nothing except the clothes on my back, my old clunker of a car, and a beat-up motorcycle. That was all I owned. My alcoholic mind was also dealing with a new reality. Before, I was constantly on the move, spending every minute of every day planning on drinking and how to get drunk. Now, that was gone, too.

I had known when returning home that I could get the help I needed if I was serious about my drinking problem. Active members of Alcoholics Anonymous (AA), my parents had both gotten sober and offered to help me do the same. They told me, "You can't do this on your own. You need to go to a meeting."

A few nights later, I drove to an Alcoholics Anonymous meeting and immediately wanted to leave. I remember walking through the door of a church where the meeting was held. I was 18 years old, skinny, disheveled, with long hair. My chest was tight, I could not breathe, and I couldn't identify what I was feeling. However, I wasn't angry.

Walking into the church through a side door, everything in me wanted to run away. I followed the arrows to the AA meeting, paralyzed in fear and overwhelmed with anxiety. However, I didn't know and wasn't able to identify what these feelings were. Emotionally, I was incompetent. I was numb.

Walking in, I saw several tables arranged in a rectangle, with chairs around them. I sat down in an empty one, looked up, and saw a bunch of "old guys." The meeting began with the Serenity Prayer, but I never said a word. No one spoke to me during or after the meeting because I came in late and missed the part where everybody introduced themselves by first name only. My brain was going so fast that I did not hear what was said or remember anything that happened. Thinking back on it now, I don't think I would have physically been able to speak if asked because, at this point, I was only four or five days sober. I'm sure most of those in the meeting were shocked to see such a young guy in their meeting.

The minute the meeting was over, I bolted out of the church and drove home. It never occurred to me to go to a bar or find a drinking buddy. I just wanted to go home. This was a profound change for me, as my whole life and identity revolved around drinking.

"How was it?" my mom asked when I got home. "What do you think?"

I lied, telling her what she wanted to hear, and returned to the basement, thinking only of my mantra. "To drink was to die." That was a phrase I had heard years ago while attending an Alateen meeting. One day, a speaker from AA made that statement in one of those meetings, and it stuck with me. "To drink was to die" was now my new mantra, knowing that if I continued drinking, it would kill me.

But being stuck with myself and not covering it up with chemicals was totally different. Suddenly, I was experiencing feelings, but they were foreign to me. I was not able to process or even identify them. I was alone in this battle. I never talked or tried bargaining with God during this time, as I was still pretty much an atheist. Nor did I ever say, "If you get me out of this, I'll never do this again." Despite quitting drinking cold turkey, I had no physical withdrawals or DTs, as others often did. By God's grace, I never experienced any of that. So, I stayed in the house for the entire week, with no one to call or talk to until the next meeting. It was the longest week of my life.

I returned the following week to the same meeting location in West Fargo, where I saw the same people smoking and drinking coffee as they had done the previous week. Although I was still scared, returning was a bit easier because I knew what to expect. I sat down at the table and looked around as the meeting started. We went around the room and introduced ourselves. When it was my turn, I spoke up.

"Hi, my name is Tim, and I'm an alcoholic."

Who said that? I thought as I tried to suck the words back in, but there it was. I said it out loud for the world to hear, but it sounded strange coming out of my mouth. I didn't say another word that night, and I don't remember much after that, but I did return to that same meeting next week. I was now three weeks sober.

One thing I noticed when attending the meetings was everyone there was older than me. One guy noticed me and, in fact, had been staring at me for three straight weeks. It was beginning to piss me off. I think he was annoyed by my silence, and he finally confronted me the third week while I was talking about my dad being in recovery.

His name was Henry, but he went by "Bud" and was also one of the meeting founders. He interrupted me and said, "You haven't drunk enough to earn a seat in this meeting, young man!"

Bud and I would go at it, and I think it was his way of making me mad enough to motivate me to sobriety. Almost anyone else would have left in anger and gotten drunk. But for some reason, I didn't. Today, you take someone aside and speak privately with them before or after the meeting. You never confront an individual in front of the entire group.

Another time, Bud looked at me and said, "What the hell are you even doing in my meeting? I've spilled more alcohol than you've drunk."

"Listen, old man," I retorted, "if you hadn't spilled so much fucking alcohol, you would have gotten here years earlier."

Bud continued provoking me, but eventually, we became the best of friends right up until the day he died.

Although I was going to meetings, I was struggling and had no idea what the people in AA were talking about. My mom had gotten me a copy of "Alcoholics Anonymous," also known as the Big Book, which is the primary text for the program and includes the 12 steps of recovery. But my mind was so screwed up I could not remember or process what I was reading. I would go to meetings and drive home scared and sober, with nothing positive in my life to replace the addiction. I needed guidance and direction because it just did not make any sense. So, I began talking to my mom more. She worked at an in-patient treatment center at St. John's, a local hospital. She asked me if I would be interested in going to their 30-day recovery program. "Yes," I said, feeling deep down that if I wanted full recovery, I had to learn how to live differently. At this point in my life, I could not relate to anything having to do with the 12 Steps, God, or any meaning or direction. I knew the First Step, "We admitted we were powerless over alcohol and that our lives had become unmanageable," but that was about the only thing that made any sense. I had nowhere to go, nothing to do, and no responsibilities. I needed to take my next step.

8

ST. JOHN'S

Prairie-St. John's in Fargo is the largest facility of its kind in North Dakota or Minnesota. Its 30-day inpatient residential treatment program provides a safe, structured living environment for patients who need continual care as they begin breaking the cycle of substance abuse and start their new life of recovery. I certainly fit that criterion.

As I mentioned, my mom was a secretary for the director of the recovery floor for alcoholics, and she was able to get me into the program. The residential treatment program is designed to allow patients time to focus on various behavioral and emotional issues that need resolution. The program staff guides the application of recovery skills, including emotional functioning, family dynamics, personal responsibility, work and school reintegration, and relapse prevention. Of course, I knew none of this going in. All I understood was that I needed to find a way to live a new life that did not include alcohol.

Entering St. John's was pretty much a blur and felt like an out-of-body experience happening to someone else. I remember the staff filling out the paperwork to check me in. Every impulse within me was to turn around and run out of there, but I knew that was not an option. I didn't know what to expect as the door closed behind me. The staff told me about two large rooms containing eight beds each. These were used for new patients they expected would be going through drug or alcohol withdrawals, with all the related physical side effects. Since I had not used drugs or alcohol recently, thankfully, I did not have to go to one of these rooms. I do remember passing by and seeing people in there, though. One man was having seizures while going through withdrawals. That mental picture still burns in my memory.

I was scared on the inside, but none of my reactions showed on the outside. I projected the image of a cool 18-year-old pretending to be tough, which was my coping mechanism. The staff told me about the facility's layout, consisting of multiple floors and meeting rooms.

"What do you mean, meeting rooms?" I asked.

They told me that treatment consisted of multiple meetings a day with different staff members. I wasn't happy about that. They also mentioned where I would be sleeping. The facility had individual "dorm" rooms with two people per room. I requested a single room, so I didn't have to talk to anybody. They took me to a room and proceeded to go through my entire suitcase, looking for drugs and alcohol. I was surprised and asked, "Why?"

"You'd be surprised what people try to bring in here," the staff member replied.

The room was small, with two beds. I discovered that asking for my own room automatically meant I got a roommate. Upon entering, I immediately encountered this old guy sitting on the other bed. I'm guessing he was in his 60s. I got settled in, and he pissed me off for some reason. I didn't like how he talked because his voice sounded like nails on a chalkboard.

I was only in the room for a couple of hours when I realized I couldn't stay with this guy. I left and went to one of the common areas on another floor, where I saw a couch partially obscured by the haze of cigarette smoke. It seemed that everyone there smoked, so I joined them but didn't talk to anyone. Then, I started getting angry and confronted one of the staff members.

"Listen, I can't be in a room with this guy," I told him, speaking of my new roommate, James.* "I thought we talked about this and that I was getting my own room," I added.

"You're going to be in the room with him. You just have to work it out," I was told.

I stormed out and went to the dining room for dinner, where I ate the bland hospital food before returning to the common area. Everything was a blur, and I wondered what was happening. My intake packet contained a copy of the AA Big Book, so I read some of it but still didn't understand much. Right before bed, the staff gave me a paper with my schedule for the next day. It told me when I had to be up, where I needed to be, and when. Structure and a schedule were totally new to me, and I was offended when they started laying out these rules and responsibilities for me. For example, on the first day, they gave me the responsibility of making the coffee in the morning. Everybody drank coffee, so it needed to start brewing in the big pot by 7:00. It took 20 to 25 minutes to complete the brew cycle on time as the residents began showing up for breakfast. If the coffee wasn't finished on time, there was hell to pay from the residents.

Rules, I thought, what the F is this? It created more stress, and I would wake up at night with anxiety attacks.

What the hell did I do? I asked myself about my decision to enter St. John's.

I was not used to living by a schedule. So, of course, I overslept the next morning and missed breakfast. Worse than that, nobody was there to start the coffee, and two people showed up pounding on my door and swearing at me because I didn't make the coffee. When I showed up to get something to eat, I was politely told that the kitchen was closed until lunch. I became adamant about getting something to eat and cursed out the poor staff member. The rules were the rules, though, and I didn't get breakfast. That was my introduction to the concept of living with rules and consequences.

The second day, the coffee was a half-hour late, and I caught more flak from the residents. My solution was to con my mom, who came into work at 6:30, to start the coffee for me, solving my problem but confusing everyone else. They couldn't figure out why the coffee was suddenly on time (and early) while I was still sleeping. After a few days, the staff caught on, my mom got busted, and they confronted me for manipulating her. I also got relieved of coffee duty.

"We're firing you because all of these people deserve someone who will take better care of them to get right the one thing they enjoy," I was told.

Unlike other in-treatment programs, we did not receive any one-on-one counseling. Our meetings usually involved a group sitting in a circle and discussing our feelings. One of the tools the staff used was a "feelings wheel" to help identify what we were experiencing. We had to talk about how specific incidents made us feel. I was clueless, and for the first few meetings, I had a cluster of feelings and could never narrow it down to one. Plus, I had trouble identifying or labeling each emotion.

All of this "feelings talk" began opening up stuff inside of me, making me feel like I was out of control. I was scared, frustrated, and experienced something similar to anxiety attacks because I didn't know how to process it all. Part of it was my rebellious mindset, which was 100 percent against authority. Now, all of that was being challenged.

As if the feelings wheel wasn't bad enough, they soon switched to "feeling flip cards." The group facilitator would go around the circle from patient to patient, holding up a card with an emotion. You had to identify the feeling and something in your life that reflected that emotion. It was horrible, and I was so paranoid that I would start counting down how many people there were in the circle until they got to me. I was so afraid I wouldn't know the emotion on the card when my turn came. The first two weeks of these meetings were stressful and added to my anxiety.

In addition to the group meetings, I was also required to take a rotation in the eight-bed "detox" room, watching the newbies come in. We sometimes had to hold the person down while they were going through withdrawal. For me, it was another "scared-straight" moment. I did not want to be 20 years older (as most of these guys were) and going through what they were experiencing. Coupled with all of this was the fact that no one was close to my age. Without knowing it, I was at the forefront of younger people getting help in AA with their alcohol addiction. This was atypical at the time, as it was more common for only older people to attend AA meetings before this time. That trend really took off in the 1980s.

I don't want to make it sound like my time at St. John's was all bad because I experienced several breakthrough moments. One profound thing happened when I was sitting at the end of the hall in one of the common areas, smoking a cigarette and drinking a cup of coffee. It was there that I remember feeling safe for the first time in my life. Ever.

No one can hurt me right now and get to me, I thought.

While this may not sound like much, it was such a profound feeling and one I could identify and appreciate. It represented an emotional breakthrough and a significant turning point for me only two weeks into the program. The best way to explain it is to finally have a true sense of safety when you have never had that. It was a wonderful feeling.

Something else happened after experiencing my feelings of safety. I discovered I subconsciously started embracing a schedule and showed up when and where I was supposed to. I wasn't fighting it anymore, which was again different for me. Admittedly, part of it was me still playing the game to finish my 30-day program. Even with my breakthroughs, I knew I needed the entire month of treatment.

One day, I heard my name over the loudspeaker and was told I needed to go to a specific room and meet with a counselor. When

I arrived, three chairs were set up: one for me, one for James, the roommate I despised, and one for the counselor.

"I understand you two are having problems," the counselor began.

"What would ever make you think that?" I asked, surprised by his question since I hadn't said anything to anyone about my roommate issues.

But it turns out James had been narcing me out daily over how I treated him, which was me being an asshole and doing things to annoy him. I didn't like him and justified my behavior.

"Let's talk through it because we need to get past this," the counselor said. "What does James say that bothers you?"

Oh, God, I thought. *I don't want to talk about this.*

I immediately shut down emotionally, went back into my survivor mode, and lashed out. Anything he did or said just irritated me, I told both of them. A short time after our meeting, James was discharged after finishing his 30 days, and I had the whole dorm room to myself. As I reflected on his departure, I realized (not knowing I was doing so) that I had shut everyone else out and fallen back into my survival mode. That led to me talking about my past and how I felt about not being safe and feeling vulnerable. By the end of the second week, I felt badly about how I had treated James. I identified that feeling as remorse. That was the first time I can ever remember feeling remorse and identifying it as such. Up until then, I lived for Tim and never thought about anyone else or their feelings. This episode was another turning point for me in identifying and dealing with my feelings. By the way, I never saw James again, so I had to learn to accept how I treated him and move on.

*Pseudonym chosen for anonymity

9

GINO

Halfway into my month-long stay at St. John's, the staff started loosening the reins on residents, trusting us more, and giving us additional freedom. For example, during our 30-minute breaks, we could leave the building, walk across the street, and enjoy the September beauty of the park that we had only seen from our windows.

I remember going over there, leaning against a tree trunk, and enjoying the warm sunshine and blue skies. I reflected on my previous life and the days ahead. It was somewhat unsettling not knowing where I was going, but comforting realizing I needed to move forward and not return to where I had been before entering treatment.

Several volunteers came to St. John's and took three or four people from the program to AA meetings. That's where I met Gino. He was in his 30s and seemed slightly off. I later found out he had some alcohol-induced brain damage but could still work and function. He was a crazy, nice guy who drove a huge Cadillac. I swear, it had a large enough backseat to hold a meeting! He would drop by and hang out with those of us going through treatment and talk about our recovery program. He latched on to me for some reason, and we spent hours talking about everything under the sun. He was a goofball and someone I never would have picked to hang out with. He started following me around constantly, almost like my shadow, and I didn't like that. It started bugging me, because I was still very much a loner. It seemed that everywhere I went, Gino was there.

He would sit in on our groups and start talking to us about what we thought our life after St. John's would be like. He said we needed to commit to attending 90 meetings in 90 days after we were released.

"Ninety meetings in 90 days. Are you crazy?" I countered. "Who has time to do that?"

Gino looked at me and said, "Well, what else have you got going on?"

The question stopped me in my tracks. I had nothing going on, and we both knew it.

"If you're serious about your recovery, you ought to make the commitment," he said. "Just like you used to put drugs and alcohol first, now you need to put AA first. If you want to grow up, you need to grow up in AA. They have all your answers for now."

I always felt Gino was talking directly to me, and years later, I found out he was. Gino was one of those guys that I didn't want hanging around me, but missed when he was gone. He was one of the few people who showed an interest in me, cared for me, and challenged me.

One day, I remember standing at the window in our common area, looking outside at the trees, and being overcome by waves of fear. I was going to be released soon and had nowhere to go and nothing to do. I had learned to be safe and sober at St. John's, but "out there" was scary. For the first time in my life, I would have to accept humanity the way they are, acting and interacting with people without my crutch of alcohol or the safety net of St. John's. The thought petrified me.

"You can't call or go around the people you used to be with," Gino said. "It's a slippery slope because you will be around people with alcohol, and it's easy to slip."

What he said was both simplistic and profound.

On the day I was released from treatment, Gino picked me up and dropped me off at home.

"Well, I'll be back at 7:00. Got an 8:00 meeting tonight," he said as he pulled into the driveway.

"Gino, I'm not going tonight. I just got home and want to get settled in."

"I'll be here at 7:00," he reiterated, unwilling to take no for an answer. "Just come out here to the car at 7:00," he continued as if he never heard me.

I couldn't believe his persistence, which really annoyed me.

What an asshole, I thought.
As Gino drove off, I walked down the driveway to the house. I turned the doorknob to the side door. It was locked.

What the hell, I thought. *I didn't even know we had a key to this house.*

I knocked on the door, and my mom answered. I put my bag down.

"Let's sit down at the table," she said.

We sat down, and Mom began. "Alright, here are the house rules. Here is a key for the house," she began. "We're going to start keeping it locked. We're giving you a key to this house, and we want you to know you will lose this key if you go back out using or drinking. You will not be allowed to live here. You will be locked out of the house and have to figure it out on your own. If you keep sober, keep going to AA meetings, and get a job, you can continue to live here."

I was bummed out and surprised by the new house rules because we had never had any before. Somehow, I had the strange idea that because I was sober and had gone to treatment, people (including my family) would trust me again and forget about the past.

But my mom learned from many years in Al-Anon and finally realized she had to set rules and boundaries for me, as well as for her and my dad, to stop enabling my behavior. Part of that was protecting their own recoveries. But I still didn't know what a boundary was, even though they had set some at St. John's, and I had learned that boundaries were necessary to protect me and put myself first in a positive way. Despite all that, I still did not fully understand the concept.

That evening, at 7:00, I heard the "honk, honk" of a car horn. It was Gino.

I went outside.

"Gino, I'm not going tonight."

"What have you got to do?" he asked, walking around to open the passenger door. "Do you want to stay sober or go back out? He asked.

"I want to stay sober."

"Then, get your ass into that car!"

I was shocked because he had never spoken to me that way.

I got in his Cadillac, and we went to the meeting. This happened every night, seven days a week. He would pull into the driveway and honk the horn to take me to the 8:00 meeting.

Gino saved my life, and by helping me, he was also working hard on his own sobriety. This was his service work in AA, something he could do to help others just by showing up and being a friend.

Every night when the meeting was over, he'd round up several other people, and we'd go for coffee and to talk. It was the same routine every night and gave me a new sense of purpose because I had nothing else to do during the day. But I knew I had the 8:00 meeting to look forward to.

At one of those "meetings after the meeting," I learned how to set a boundary. A guy I had put on a pedestal because he had 15 years of recovery drew three circles on the backside of the paper placemat. He told me I had to set boundaries before letting people into my inner circle of trust.

"People start in your outer circle," he explained, "and gradually move in as they gain your trust."

For me, this was a slow but effective way of setting boundaries with other people. When people betrayed my trust, I got angry and recognized it as a betrayal. Slowly, I was learning the tools that most kids learn at much younger ages.

Gino stayed in my life for years but never became my sponsor. I always heard in meetings that you should "find someone to sponsor you who has something you want," and Gino did not fit that bill. He did become my temporary sponsor, but in the long run, he turned out to be just a goofy friend that everyone in AA knew, no matter what meeting they attended. He and I attended one to three meetings a week for the next seven or eight years.

Gino and I completed the 90 meetings in 90 days challenge after I left St. John's, which was hard for me, even though I had nothing else to do. But it turned out to be a huge step in recognizing how deadly alcoholism is. It is a progressive disease. I soon realized that for me, "to drink is to die." Remember my mantra in life. There is no logical reason I should have gotten sober at 18 and stayed sober all these years. I feel God chose me to deliver this message, and I genuinely believe I am a walking miracle by His grace.

10

IN STEEL BEAM WE TRUST

Gino's service work was helping others, especially getting them to meetings and encouraging them to keep reading the Big Book. Although that "encouragement" occasionally annoyed me, it was exactly what I needed at the time. It kept me believing in the meetings, but not necessarily in God. I would tune out the "God part" during meetings while paying attention to the teachings about finding someone who had what you wanted and asking them to be your sponsor.

For me, that ended up being Bud, who became my AA sponsor. Even though he had initially been a pain in my ass, I chose him because he had been sober for a long time and was consistently attending meetings, plus I think I trusted him. I say "I think" because I still had trust issues. During our AA meetings, I kept hearing about a "spiritual awakening," "spiritual feelings," and making amends. I began meeting weekly with Bud, who encouraged me to read the AA Big Book. Of course, I played him, lied, and told him I had read such and such. On the positive side, I continued attending many meetings and saw who came regularly and those who disappeared. The latter scared me, as it did when people slipped and confessed to messing up. I did not want to go down that path. I didn't feel like I had another "drunk" in me.

I was always anxious during the meetings, especially when we sat in a circle. I would get nervous when it came time to speak; it took me years to get over that. The format of every meeting consisted of choosing someone to read the different elements of the AA program. I was so nervous about reading in front of someone. It brought back shame over my lack of education, having quit school in the tenth grade. One of my coping techniques was memorizing the different elements, like the 12 steps, "How it Works," etc. When it came to my turn, I would act like I was reading the page, but I was reciting it from memory. It was the easiest way to get by and accomplish my goal of not being embarrassed. Keep in mind that I still only existed to go to meetings because I had no job or anything else to do.

Speaking of jobs, one of the few "formal" jobs I ever had, besides Mo's, was working as a busboy at Bonanza Steakhouse when I was about 14. I went in for the interview and was told I had to cut my long hair, which I never did. Instead, I stuffed it inside my hat, making it look like I had cut it. I made it about eight or nine days before showing up drunk and getting fired. Before that job, I helped build motorcycles overnight with a friend, drinking all night while assembling the bikes from the manufacturer. We would unpack the crates and build the bikes, and I got paid per completed bike.

Fast forward to being in recovery at 18 and still not understanding the real concept of work and schedules. Plus, I had the usual rebellion that comes with being a teenager. I would tell everyone I was "raised" in AA and learned about functioning in life during our meetings and get-togethers, as well as hanging out with others in the program. They modeled all this "normal" life stuff for me without realizing it. Things most people learn growing up in a family.

Finally, the time came for me to get a job, so I found one working in a warehouse from 7:00 a.m. to 3:00 p.m. In typical Tim fashion, I would show up an hour late and get my butt chewed out. I didn't see it as a big deal, but to them, it was. As you might guess, I got fired in about a week and had to go to my AA meetings and explain what happened. Next, was a job as a parts runner for a car company. Same thing. I was late all the time. The job was within walking distance from my house, so how could I be late? Then, one day, my manager took me aside.

"Listen, these parts have to be there on time, or our mechanic can't work," he said. "I'm pulling you off of being a parts runner, and you're going to work with me in the Parts Department as an assistant parts guy."

"Is this a promotion?" I naively asked him, being clueless about the work environment.

"No, this is no promotion. It's a demotion!" he answered incredulously.

My problem was I would go to my meetings, stay late at the "meeting after the meeting, drink coffee until midnight, and have trouble getting up to arrive at work on time. I thought I was taking responsibility for my recovery when the "responsible" thing would have been to go to bed on time and get up for work. Consequently, I got fired and couldn't understand why. It finally dawned on me that they meant it when they said to be somewhere on time!

They all started laughing at my revelation when I told my AA group this.

I started to understand that I needed to follow society's rules rather than, "Tim's rules."

I continued getting sober, collecting my milestone sobriety chips, and watching others talk about their years of sobriety, thinking, *there's no way I can do that.* But the more I showed up, the more I saw other people's progress and how consistency in recovery paid off. I saw people walk in destitute, and six months later, they were totally different. Despite that, I could not see my own progress. I finished Step One with no problem but got totally stuck on the "higher power" concept of steps Two and Three.

"Why are you hung up on that," a group member asked me.

"I just don't believe in God," I responded. "Why would I be here if God is real?" I asked. "If he is real, he is a punishing God, and why would I believe in him?"

"Don't call your higher power 'God,'" one group member told me. "Make it something, anything, more powerful than you. Is that steel beam over there more powerful than you?" he asked me, pointing to a beam in the church.

So, my first "higher power" became that steel beam, as something more powerful than myself.

"Be thankful for your sobriety for that day," group members told me. It was the cliché "one-day-at-a-time" mentality, but it worked. "I can do this one day at a time and not drink today" became my daily "prayer."

My "belief" gradually rested in the group and its power in keeping me sober and through what I saw there and during the meetings after the meeting. There, we would talk about ourselves, our progress, and how others were doing. During this period, younger people were coming into recovery, and I began hanging out with them. Suddenly, I wasn't the "newbie" but the recovery "veteran" in these groups of people, helping others just beginning the program. While I recognized I was mentoring others, it scared me because I was so fear-based. But I gave them advice and talked about what had kept me sober, unknowingly following my mentor in helping others.

As part of mentoring others, I talked with them about service work, such as arriving early and setting up chairs, posting the flyers in the parking lot, or making coffee before others showed up. This also taught me "life" responsibilities, which I struggled with in a job situation. I also knew I didn't need to rush into completing the 12 steps. I realized I needed to "live" the steps, not just "work" them.

Another turning point came one night when I met Bob L. in a meeting. After the meeting in Morehead, he approached me.

"Listen, young man, if you're serious about a job, and you're serious about sobriety and working the steps, I have a job for you." Bob owned E.W. Wylie, a trucking company, and I went to work for him. I started as a truck washer in Fargo in the winter, where it was 20 degrees below zero. We worked in a cold building, spray washing the trucks in frigid conditions. It was horrible, but I learned a bunch of different jobs at this facility. Surprisingly, I showed up on time because I didn't want to disappoint Bob. I respected him; this was the first time I recognized someone who valued and took an interest in me and gave me a chance. Suddenly, I learned a work ethic that would become a focal point in my life. Bob was my motivation for that, even though he worked in the business office, and I was one of the worker bees.

It was the first time in my life I gave a damn about working and showing up on time. I went from a truck washer to a "grunt" or "gofer" for the shop guys. That got me out of washing trucks! I worked hard, outworking everyone else, and became a parts runner for Gino, who, ironically, was my manager. That was both a good and bad thing. Even though I was sober, learning responsibility, and being productive, I was still a master manipulator. So, I started working Gino to make things easier and softer for me by asking him to do things instead of treating him like my boss. Despite this, I got promoted to the operations side of the trucking business as a dispatcher. This was when truck dispatching was just beginning, so I was in the right place at the right time. I had to help find loads for drivers to haul and other odd jobs. I worked harder than my colleagues, even though I was only 19. I worked for E.W. Wylie for 11 years.

II

WHITE OUTS

During this time in my life, I started developing relationships with girls. Previously, I had only hooked up with a girl when I was drunk but had never had any connection when sober. While attending meetings, I met an 18-year-old woman who lived at a halfway house and was a newcomer to the AA program. I was 19 at the time when Connie and I started "meeting" dating and seeing each other on weekends, even though AA recommends not dating or getting into a relationship with someone newly sober. Although I knew nothing about relationships or dating, the two of us really got along and eventually were together all the time. She was my best friend, and although I was not in love with her, we eventually got married. We stayed sober together but did not know what we wanted in the relationship except to remain sober. Being young and naïve, we thought we knew everything but, in reality, lived separate lives and were clueless about making a marriage work.

At work, I kept progressing in the company, eventually becoming the boss of the Transportation Division. I was self-taught, learning about life and responsibility from others in the AA program. Every Friday, several people from my AA group met for lunch at Mr. Steak. They were making major decisions in life, such as college choices out of town or just graduating and getting into the workforce. Still, I felt like I wasn't making progress.

I'm going nowhere; I'm a tenth-grade dropout, I thought, even though I was rapidly rising in my company. I couldn't see my own success. I felt like it was never enough, and I wasn't "good" enough.

Spiritually, I still struggled with the AA third step, the so-called "God" step. Simply stated, it says we "Made a decision to turn our will and our lives over to the care of God *as we understood Him*." I did not understand God or how He fits into my life, but I was okay with the "as we understood him" concept. Then, one night, I was scheduled to speak at a meeting in Moorhead, Minnesota, as I had finally grown comfortable speaking in front of other people. I noticed the picture on the wall behind the guy speaking before me.

It had been there for years, but I suddenly saw the picture of a ship on the ocean and a young boy steering it. God had a hand on the boy's shoulder, pointing the way and guiding him. That simple moment became a turning point in my relationship with God. I finally understood the guiding hand concept and began understanding the "turning things over to God" idea found in Step 3, which I was able to complete with an area pastor's help.

That itself is a funny story. I had joined a skeet shooting club with a bunch of program guys, and the conversation turned to God. One of my AA friends felt I was putting off doing my Step 3 work, and after some prodding from him, I decided I had to do it. I got into my car, intending to return to the apartment I shared with my wife. I prayed for the courage to follow through with my commitment to meet with a pastor in Moorhead to work on my third step.

Suddenly, I realized I had what I called a "whiteout" (as opposed to the blackouts I used to have) and missed my exit to go home. Instead, I exited the freeway and was heading to the Moorhead church! It was definitely a God thing, as I just showed up without an appointment. I met up with the clergyman who helped me complete the third step, and then went home with a new sense of peace I never had before. Once we got through the third step, we talked about a personal relationship with God. Thanks to that turning point, I have a strong spiritual connection with my higher power today. From that moment came opportunities to talk to youth groups and share parts of my story about addiction.

Despite my sobriety and growth in AA, I still struggled with other issues, such as money. At times, I wondered if life would ever get any easier. My life had changed radically in just two years, but I was putting a lot of pressure on myself, deep-rooted in my lack of self-worth. I knew I needed to get counseling to dig deep into my self-worth challenges and clear up some lingering issues from my childhood, while trying to better myself, which I did in every area except my marriage. By this time, I had risen to be a company sales rep, so I began traveling a lot. To afford the travel, I had to fly out on Sunday and return on Friday. This started my business travel life but was death to a relationship, which I didn't realize at the time. Connie and I lived independently, working, and then keeping busy with our individual projects. I also attended one to three AA meetings weekly, but we never attended the same meeting. Consequently, we had no time together and drifted further apart.

Connie was a high school counselor when she began having lunch with a guy who was also in AA. I knew him but didn't really like him because he had a reputation for preying on women. I later found out that Connie was, in fact, having an affair with him. Bob L. had heard that Connie and I were having problems, and he thought I was the one who was up to something. I remember he drove to my house and chewed me out and didn't believe me when I told him the truth.

Meanwhile, after ten years at E.W. Wylie, I knew I had plateaued professionally and needed to advance my career. So, I applied for a job at Yellow Freight, and they offered me a position making twice as much as I made at Wylie. Still, giving my notice at Wylie was one of the hardest and most emotional things I have ever done after giving them my heart, life, and soul. It was cutting the umbilical cord and ending something that was also a big part of my sobriety. E.W. Wylie had taken a chance on me and helped me develop professionally. But Yellow Freight saw more potential in me. I wanted to achieve more and knew I could succeed at a different level, including making more money, one of my goals.

While leaving the security of the AA-related job at Wylie was scary, Yellow Freight represented a wonderful opportunity. I would not fly for business as much but would be responsible for a three-state area by car. The change gave me a more predictable schedule for when I would be home. Despite having more free time, I didn't use any of it to build my relationship with my wife but added other things to do. Life began improving financially, and in my spare time, my brother and I started fixing up cars and selling them.

Life went on, and I enjoyed some financial success, but it was obvious that my marriage wasn't working. While Connie and I loved each other, we weren't in love with each other. And it didn't help that with all my activities, I was never home. I knew Connie and I should separate but didn't have the guts to act. We were married for 14 years when the inevitable happened. She filed for divorce. Our relationship together, friends, and much of our social life revolved around AA, so for me, it was more than just my marriage ending. It affected a lot of other things in my life as well. I worked for someone in AA at Wylie, married someone in AA, and continued attending AA meetings. The program was at the center of my world. In addition, the life skills I had developed and my spiritual growth, so far had all come through Alcoholics Anonymous.

Suddenly, all the legs of my three-legged stool (work, marriage, and friends) were being kicked out from under me. Although this was a huge setup for a relapse, I didn't go down that path; instead, I turned to people in the program for strength, courage, and counseling. We would talk, and I would feel better, but emotionally, going through a divorce was a three-year paralyzing rollercoaster for me. During those three years, I went through the motions of life, moment-by-moment, and survived day by day. Although I never came close to falling off the wagon, I didn't know if I would be mentally okay. I wondered if I could live this way with all the pain. Surprisingly, I never considered suicide.

During those tough times, my sobriety remained stable, and I saw many miracles as new people came into our meetings and turned their lives around. These were very encouraging to me, considering what I was going through. I worked and went to meetings every day. Connie and I were apart for about a year between separation and divorce, and I still had no clue about dating. We got back together briefly, and she apologized for making a mistake. Still, deep down inside, I knew we couldn't get back together. She pursued reconciling for many years, but I never wanted to go back there. I knew we weren't meant to be married and had outgrown each other.

Coming out on the other side, I knew I had learned and gained so much wisdom and looked at life differently. *Bring it on* was my new mantra, knowing I could handle a lot after surviving a divorce. I now had so much more to offer others, especially in the program.

I remember early on in my sobriety, thinking there was no reason at age 18 that I should be sober. For whatever reason, God lifted that urge to drink from me, and it never came back. I learned that "pain is the touchstone to spiritual growth," and that was something I was living. There were times I would get stuck in my head and see others living their lives, but eventually, I realized there is life after divorce. In recovery, I never quit going to meetings. Those meetings saved my life and got me through many tough times. I lost myself in AA, and it became my identity, helping me grow up and teaching me how to be a responsible, mature adult.

12

LOST AND FOUND

All of my feelings were magnified after the divorce, and everything involved was tied to my sobriety, which was scary. When the reality of the divorce sunk in, I was sitting in my tiny two-bedroom house all alone. Everything there reminded me of Connie and our lives together. The memories triggered the pain, even though I had wanted the divorce as well. Once the marriage was over, I began my journey of finding an identity.

At that point, I decided to sell the house, thinking it would give me a sense of relief from the bitter memories. I moved into a townhouse with Dusty, my cocker spaniel companion and best friend. I had gotten custody of him in the divorce with the agreement that Connie would occasionally take him on outings and such. The move to a tri-level dwelling was a simple one. I would share my new home with my friend, Mike, one of my AA sponsors. Mike was working toward becoming an addiction counselor and came and went a lot. For me, it was a great arrangement. The move was a small step toward discovering a broader identity than existing within the AA world and living in the "real world," as I perceived it. Although I knew splitting up with Connie was the right thing to do, the pain level was intense, even with the move and the changes I was making in my life.

I was going through the motions of life while continuing to work at Yellow Freight. Some days, I drove around aimlessly in between appointments or after work. I had to find a new goal in my life, but, of course, one that did not involve drinking. In some way, it paralleled my old way of life, but without the drinking. While I was dealing with the emotional turmoil from the divorce, Bud passed away, adding to my grief. Many people came alongside me to help with that. However, I still tended to isolate myself, again going back to an old, familiar pattern—this time without the booze.

The pain was so intense at times, like another out-of-body experience. Mike and I lived together for a few years in the townhouse. I continued working at Yellow Freight, succeeding as frequently the top sales guy, even though I was in a smaller market than many colleagues. Through that success, the company began talking to me about taking the next step by moving to a larger market, like Minneapolis, or helping develop and write the sales program, techniques, and training for all Yellow Freight salespeople.

I merely existed in Fargo and was alone most of the time. I had never dated anyone, even though I was now in my 30s. Remember, I met Connie at an AA meeting, socialized with her, and got married. As I began to reach out to others to help me deal with my pain, Daryl came into my life through AA. He was a Godsend in helping me develop to the next level. As time passed, the pain began easing. Suddenly, I had a new set of experiences and tools in my toolbox to share while working with others in recovery. I began realizing I would be okay and would not start using again despite the pain. While I knew I had made some progress and changed, my direction in life was still uncertain. I had a job but needed a career track. Through my conversations with Daryl, I knew I needed to go out on my own, and starting my own business was something I wanted to do. However, I didn't want to be involved in trucking or transportation. But what would my business be? This is where Daryl's wisdom and business success came into play.

"You know what I've learned in life," he said, "if you want to do something, it's best to do something you know." Which, of course, was trucking.

"Listen," Daryl continued, "all of the work you've done at Wylie and elsewhere, you've been making everybody else successful when you could be making yourself successful."

What he said went over my head because of my low self-esteem, but it stayed nestled in the recesses of my mind.

During this time, my roommate Mike had gotten serious with a girl, and the guy who owned the townhouse was ready to sell it. I had no interest in buying it because something inside me knew that I would be tied to Fargo if I did so. So, it was time for another move.

Amid this, Connie called and wanted to take Dusty to the lake with her family one weekend. I thought that was a great idea and decided to go to a motorcycle race with friends. Suddenly, my old Motorola brick-sized cell phone rang. It was Connie, crying uncontrollably. Dusty had died suddenly from over-exertion after an aneurysm burst in his brain. I was stunned and devastated. My best friend was instantly gone. You see, I wasn't interacting much with my parents or siblings during this time, so it was just Dusty and me. The pain of Dusty's death was worse than my divorce and sent me to a deep, dark place of depression. But I didn't turn to alcohol and instead leaned on friends and people in AA to help me through. Stunningly, I never had an overwhelming urge to drink during this dark time.

Dusty's death served as another turning point in my life. I moved out of the townhouse and into a one-bedroom apartment. I was a mess on the inside while looking successful on the outside. That was me, walking down the street. People thought I had it together, but inside, it was a different story. While I was working the AA program, I felt God was preparing me for something bigger, using each of these events for something else, although I couldn't see it at the time. Even after the divorce, I knew there was something better on the other side. Whenever, whatever, or wherever that was. If I just got up, dressed up, and showed up, I knew something good would happen for me.

Wow, here I am, I thought one day, looking out my third-floor balcony window, pondering what the future held. I had no idea but began trying to create a life for myself. I joined a local gym and was either there, at work, or going to a meeting. I had never been alone in my life. It was another opportunity to learn to live alone, be comfortable with and function by myself. Through this time, I started talking to girls and figuring out what a date was, although I had no self-confidence in that arena.

I continued talking to Daryl about something more. Finally, I decided to develop a plan for my future. I began kicking around ideas related to trucking, since that was what I knew professionally, realizing Daryl was right about staying with something I knew. I asked around and found one local company that owned 12 trucks. It was for sale, and I began investigating this possibility and thought I could make it work. But I needed investors and someone to believe in me.

It was close to becoming a reality when I was in my apartment during a December snowstorm and had an OMG moment. *If I close on this business,* I thought, *I'm stuck in Fargo, North Dakota for the rest of my life. I can't do it. There is so much more out there in the world to discover.* Daryl was experiencing great success. I recognized it, so I backed out of the deal and started making tentative plans to leave Fargo.

13

TRYING MY LUCK

Looking out at the snowbank on that dreary December day, I decided to move to Las Vegas. Why Sin City, of all places? Carl, a friend and one of our customers when I was at Yellow Freight, worked for an electrical wholesale company and had taken a job transfer to Las Vegas with his company. We kept in touch. He knew I wasn't centered and needed a new direction, and he agreed that if I moved there, he would show me around and share his apartment, at least until I got settled. I was looking forward to hanging out with him as I got acclimated to life in Las Vegas. My dilemma was that everything in my safe zone was in Fargo, so stepping out and leaving all I knew was a huge risk.

I felt like I had no direction in life and no real close friends, although I had many program friends. Everything was tied to Fargo, much as it had been linked to Wylie, then to Connie. I was ripping off all these bandages when I decided to see if there was more than Fargo. But for me, the AA promises told me I could do that. At the same time, I was paralyzed with heightened anxiety and fear.

In a manner of speaking, making this decision felt like being reborn and heading for a new challenge. I went to work, figuring out all the logistics, right down to the finances, knowing I could survive without a job for a time while I got settled in my new location. Most of my friends encouraged me to go because I had no ties, such as a family, holding me back from moving. Many of them wished they could do the same, and it seemed for me to be now or never.

Carl was not an AA program person, but we still had much in common. He became the first close friend I made that was not connected to my recovery and was a Godsend in helping me take this next step. I couldn't explain why I wanted to move, but something was drawing me to do this, and I didn't know what it was. Still, it was not easy to do because I was in so much pain and fear that everything was magnified. As I boxed up my stuff and packed my car, Carl saw I was emotionally out of control, so he hopped on a plane to Fargo and drove the truck to Las Vegas with me. That is a true friend!

We loaded the rental truck with all my stuff and hooked up the tow package for the old Porsche 911 Targa I had restored. Some friends showed up to help us load and say goodbye, because we planned to leave the next day. I had already said farewell to my mom and dad. What should have been an exciting time of adventure, instead became something that triggered my anxiety. Suddenly, I turned to Carl and said, "Let's just go." Even though I had been sober for 17 years, I was still dealing with a lot of pain. That is a good reminder that even if you've been in recovery for a long time, it is a lifelong process. As a result of my anxiety, instead of enjoying the trip, we drove non-stop 1,500 miles to Las Vegas, Nevada. It took almost 24 hours, and we arrived at night. Coming out of the darkness of the mountains and seeing the bright lights of the city triggered more fear and trepidation in me instead of excitement and anticipation.

While en route to Las Vegas, Carl dropped a bombshell on me. About a year earlier, he had met a girl at church, and they started dating. Shortly before my move, they decided to move in together into Carl's apartment. In fact, it was already a done deal, and she had moved in weeks earlier. Suddenly, I had no place to live, although Carl agreed I could stay with them for a short time until I found something on my own. This added to my anxiety because I was moving with no job and now no place to live. I quickly realized I was simply trading my situation in Fargo for the same scenario in a new city without the friends or connections I had in Fargo.

We arrived in Las Vegas, and I ended up renting a one-bedroom apartment that Kim*, a friend of Carl's girlfriend, recommended. She and I began hanging out and getting to know each other. Our relationship was always a bit weird because she was secretive, and we always met up in out-of-the-way places. But she was someone to hang out with, and I was new in town, so I went with it. Nevertheless, I started getting a weird vibe about the whole thing.

One day, Kim invited me to meet her Italian family at a restaurant in the area. I said I would join her there, so I got in my beat-up Porsche 911 and began driving. The next thing I knew, I was in an industrial area, far from restaurant row. I pulled up to the address, and two stoic looking guys with their arms folded met me at the first of two wire gates.

"Can I help you," one of them asked?

I told them who I was meeting, and they got in their car and led me through the second wire gate. Arriving at the door, a third guy led me into a darkened room with several tables, red velvet walls, and a weird-colored carpet. *OMG, this is like something out of an Italian gangster movie*, I thought. *What the hell?*

When I noticed Kim wasn't there, I started getting a bad feeling about it all. She finally arrived and introduced me to her family. I knew something was going on, but I didn't know what to do.

We all sat down at four different round tables, with eight to ten people at each table, and the waitress took our order. The father gave a toast, which sounded like something out of the Sopranos. He thanked one of the cousins (the guest of honor) for bringing the family together and growing the family business. This guest of honor had expanded the businesses (mostly strip joints) into Florida and ended up in prison. I was at his welcome home dinner after getting released. The evening progressed, and I later excused myself from the dinner, saying I had to get up and go to work in the morning. I just wanted to get out of there!

After excusing myself and leaving, I drove through the gates with a feeling of relief washing over me. I headed straight to my apartment, driving faster and faster to get away from there. I never got the feeling that Kim understood or was involved in the family business. But after the experience at the dinner, I had second thoughts about seeing her. I had recurring fantasies about being sucked into the family business. I called Carl and asked him about it. He didn't know about the family because he only hung out with Kim and knew nothing about her family. I also learned what I had suspected and what you have already figured out: Kim's family was tied to organized crime and the mob. Welcome to Las Vegas, Tim!

I knew dealing with her situation and family was way out of my league, and we began talking less and less. Kim finally opened up, confessing that she cared about me but was trying to "figure stuff out" regarding her boyfriend (whom I knew nothing about). We parted amicably, and I stayed as far away from the family as possible. During all this, I was fearful that her boyfriend might come after me at some point, especially if he had ties to organized crime. After Kim, I was very lonely. I was alone at work, drove to meetings alone, and back home alone. She and I lost touch, and I never heard from her again.

From racer to team owner with a lifetime in between, I'm pictured here at one of the many race tracks around the US in 2022. Always focused & driven to win every single race.

The Arizona Super TT in April of 2023. Won by Estenson Racing's Super Twins Rider, J.D. Beach.

This was Estenson Logistics first customer of my multi-fleet trucking business in southern California in 2001. I was 43 years old and Estenson Logistics grew exponentially after this year and until we sold.

My employees wrote a short story book about their time with me at the company. It was incredibly touching. The saying on the front is what gave me the courage to start the company in 1999.

Pictured is a set of my leathers that I raced in during the 1974 & 1975 seasons, along with a Champion Framed 250cc Yamaha.

Racing a half-mile track in north Minnesota in 1974 against a Canadian rider. I was 16 years old. I did end up winning this race and can still remember how it felt.

My father, Morrie, is pictured here. After he found sobriety, he went on to become an American Flat Track (AMA) referee. This particular race was in Minnesota in 1974.

My father on the left, my sister, Marcia beside him, my brother, Mark in the middle, and me on my mom's lap. This was in our Fargo, ND home on 13th Avenue.

This is me, Dan and my brother, Mark at the Fargo, ND home on 13th Ave. We spent most of our days exploring, and building hide-outs or forts.

My brother, Mark on the left, me in the middle and my sister, Marcia on the right.

This is Cycle Race Park in Detroit Lakes, MN, where I first began my racing career at about 9 years old. This is also where my love of racing motorcycles all began.

Yes, that's fifteen-year-old me with long blond hair and my brother, Mark behind me during the AMA Novice Racing Season in 1975. I was preparing to get my novice racing license. This bike had a 360cc Yamaha engine.

This is blond me again with our friend, Craig. Mark worked here at Power Products. We were able to run our races out of their shop in Fargo, ND.

I'm with Dallas Daniels here, an Estenson racer, signed at fifteen years old. We were assessing footage during a training session. Dallas is known throughout the country as one of the most talented American Flat Track riders to date.

Two riders mid-air and off the jump at the Arizona Super TT. Estenson racers, Dallas Daniels, #32 & JD Beach, #95, were competing & won 1st & 2nd place in the race.

Estenson Racing captures both 450 & Super Twins Main Event, clean sweep in August 2024 at the Black Hills Half Mile in Rapid City, SD.

Dallas Daniels dominates the night at the Orange County Speedwas in Middleston, NY with another Main Event Win.

This was during one of our annual Alaska Fishing Trips. We would take customers & employees to celebrate the year (no work). This was shortly after we hit our 5 year mark. We did these trips every year until I sold Estenson Logistics.

"This is me with my daughter Sami at her Daddy/Daughter Dance, 'Calendar Girl'-- we were *April*."

My son Max and I having one of our many wars. Traci wasn't happy with the foam darts ending up everywhere, but these were treasured times for us both. Max is now 20 years old.

I own a couple of motorcycles. This is one of my *man caves* or airplane hangers that I use to house & display my historic collection of vintage motorcycles.

This was in 2004 in Atlanta, GA at a private fundraiser for President George W. Bush.

To Tim
Best Wishes,

This painting is titled "Christ Our Pilot" by painter Warner Sallman. Seeing this painting during an AA meeting was a pivotal moment in my life. It helped me when I was stuck to move through step three of my sobriety. I realized that while I as not 'that religious' or couldn't believe in how 'God could control my life,' I could let go and let God be my guide *the God of my understanding*.

Yes, even our pups have their own bikes. Not much of motorcycle riders though.

My wife had this photo created. The left is me in 1975 and of course, me now in 2024 on the right.

My greatest achievement. My pride and My joy. My life's most fortunate blessing — My family. My daughter Sami on the left. My wife Traci on the bike and my son Max on the right. This is one of our racing bikes that I turned into a street bike.

14

ROLLING THE DICE

I had planned on taking a couple of years off from working, but would wake up in the morning with nothing to do and nowhere to go. It was a dangerous position for an alcoholic to be in. So, I started looking in the paper for a job. I first called Yellow Freight, whom I had previously worked for. I also called another truck-related company, Truline Corporation, which was looking for a sales rep. They were interested in me, and so a few days later, I dressed up in my suit and tie and went to their "office." It was a crap-hole of trailers and a small metal building with a tiny office. All of it was covered in layers of dust. I met Paul Truman, wearing a wrinkled-up golf shirt, blue jeans, and boots.

After the formalities, he bluntly asked, "What are you doing here? You are way overqualified for this position! You have more experience than I do!"

I told him I was new in town, starting over, and needed a job. Paul and I hit it off, and he hired me right away to do sales, business development, and strategic growth planning. Unfortunately, the job paid next to nothing, about $600 a week, with no sales commission. I started the following week at my desk in the mechanic's shop, next to the toolbox, with no air conditioning, despite the intense desert heat. Part of me wanted to chuck it and return to Fargo, but I had promised myself to give it a year.

One day, I met Paul's father, Grant Truman.

"Hey Tim, let's go for a ride," he said. So, we drove for a while when he pulled into a car dealership and started looking at used cars.

"What kind of car do you want?" Grant asked me.

"What do you mean, what kind of car do I want?"

"I can't have you seeing my customers in a Porsche," he said. "You pull up in a Porsche, and people will think we don't need any business."

"I agree with you, but I can't afford a car, Grant."

"I'm buying this car for you. Just pick out the one you want."

I picked out a white Ford Explorer that was a couple of years old. Grant went inside to do the paperwork and returned to his truck, where I was sitting.

"Tomorrow, have Paul drive you over and pick up your new car," he said.

"Grant, I don't know what to say; this is just…" I responded before he interrupted.

"I have a lot of trust in you, and I don't know why because I don't trust people, but I have a good feeling about you," he said.

As we drove back through the surrounding foothills overlooking the city, it was around dinner time, and Las Vegas was lighting up. Paul pulled over and put the truck in park.

"Young man, this city can eat you alive. I am not bullshittin' you," he said. "Look at that. What do you see?"

"I see all kinds of casinos," I responded.

"That's right," he responded, "but look at all the lights. Just remember, the most important lesson I can teach you is this city isn't lit by winners. Young man, stay away from that Strip. Drive around it, but don't go inside of those casinos," he warned, imparting sound wisdom about the realities of Las Vegas' glitter and glamor.

Years later, I asked Paul why he took a risk by hiring me at Truline.

"It wasn't us taking a risk, but you were taking a risk on us because we were a very small operation. We had bumped around with various salespeople and had not had much success. Las Vegas wasn't a big trucking market, so you did not get people with much experience in either operation or sales."

Paul said I was polished, professional, and experienced, and they put me right to the test when Anheuser-Busch, one of our customers, asked us to take some loads to Texas.

Tim handled it all flawlessly," Paul said. With him on board, we were already almost immediately to start doing things we had never done before. Some of the things we did were a stretch for us, but not for him."

I later learned from Paul that Grant thought of me as a fourth son and was rooting for me to succeed. This was foreign and felt good."

I had not realized how Las Vegas might be a trap for me with my addiction tendencies. But when I started attending meetings, I quickly realized the connection between gambling and alcohol and how one can very easily lead to the other. I also learned many people got sober and lived a better life but were still hooked on the Vegas lure. Many of them did not really work their recovery.

One night, I met Charlie at an AA meeting. He was a happy-go-lucky, slightly overweight guy who lived beyond his means. We hit it off and started hanging out together. For Charlie, money was just an object. He owned a shop that made signs, banners, and such, but did not work his business very well. He didn't fulfill orders or was late when he did, which hurt his reputation. One day, he was awarded several thousand dollars, maybe as much as half a million, in a long-standing lawsuit that finally got settled.

"If I don't spend this money right away, I'm just gonna blow it," he told me. "I think I'll buy a house." That's what he did, buying a house for cash in a posh neighborhood that Hollywood stars used to live in. He started renovating the house. I would come over to hang out and help, but he would suddenly announce he had to leave while I was there.

Charlie would be gone for hours at a time, which raised red flags for me, as addicts are known for mysteriously disappearing. So, one day, I confronted him.

"Charlie, what the hell is going on?"

He told me he was chauffeuring high-dollar hookers to the casino hotels, bribing the staff, then serving as "muscle" for the girls until their "work" was through. I was speechless. "This is way out of my comfort zone," I told him. "I don't want to know anymore."

Meanwhile, six months into my Las Vegas adventure, I ran into Mike Boatman, whom I had met years ago. He had learned that I had moved to the Southwest.

"Hey, will you finally go to work for me now that you're out here?" he asked me over the phone. "I got a call about a truck leasing company that is starting a dedicated contracts division," he told me. "I think you'd be really good at this job, and I'm going to have this guy, Steve Scully, call you."

The one big problem was that the job was in Los Angeles, and I had no desire to move there. After some back-and-forth banter, Mike sweetened the deal by saying he might be able to let me live in Phoenix, which did interest me. By now, I knew I had to get out of Las Vegas. Plus, I had a friend in Phoenix.

Steve Scully and I struck a deal over the phone after he told me, "Mike Boatman speaks highly of you; I don't need to meet you." I accepted the job at Scully Distribution and then resigned from my position at Truline. This was really hard for me, because I liked Paul, and we had done some great things there. He was totally supportive of my work at Truline. I was surprised he thought so highly about my time at Truline and did not realize the impact I had had. I packed up again, got another U-Haul truck, and headed to Tempe, Arizona, a suburb of Phoenix.

Once I got to Phoenix, I learned that Charlie had lost his business, continued working with the girls, began using drugs again, and finally began dealing drugs. He eventually got killed in a drug deal gone bad. It was not surprising to me, as I saw it coming, but I was saddened by the news. The way I found out was strange. I had loaned him some money with a boat he owned as collateral. After numerous attempts to collect, I got fed up and decided to drive back to Las Vegas to claim the boat. I showed up at the house and waited a while for Charlie but eventually gave up, took the boat, and returned to Phoenix. Finally, an acquaintance told me what had happened to him.

By God's grace, I had survived my encounters with Kim, Charlie, and "the family." But on the bright side, by moving to Las Vegas, I met Paul, Grant, and Mike. Had I not met them, my life would have been totally different.

*Pseudonym chosen for anonymity**

15

TOO GOOD TO BE TRUE

I had another friend, Jim, who had moved to Phoenix, so when I knew I would be relocating, I visited him at his office in Tempe. We hung out, and he advised me where I should live and how to navigate the Phoenix area.

While there, I met a girl named Toni, working in the office next door. She had moved out of her parents' home in Scottsdale to go out on her own, and we went on several dates. Meeting Toni made my transition to Phoenix easier, and because we hit it off so well, we decided to move in together. We planned on it being temporary, but it turned out to be much more. Because of my bad experience in Las Vegas, I was looking for a flaw in Toni or a hidden lifestyle, like I had seen with Kim. I was honest with Toni about my alcoholism, and it worked out that she couldn't really afford a Scottsdale apartment. So, my moving in was a win-win.

I arrived in Phoenix to work for a start-up company with a new girlfriend and a new life. Three of the biggest stressors in life and moving, starting a new job, and beginning a new relationship, and I was doing all three at once. It was another transition, with a lot of travel flying back to California, since the truck rental and leasing company was based in Los Angeles. I was in the sales division, and part dedicated contract services, which meant clients leased the trucks, employees, etc. I was going to work hard and grow the company, and Toni was also working. What was different for me was having someone to come home to.

Going into this company, we had a plan and purpose, plus it was a start-up, so there was the rush of getting it going, and the business took off fairly quickly. I kept looking for flaws in Toni and decided to give it a year, waiting for something to show up in her life, because she seemed too perfect. We bought a small house in the Phoenix suburb of Ahwatukee and were living the American dream. It was so weird for me because there was no conflict, which I wasn't used to. I knew myself well enough to know I managed chaos well, but this was different. I went ahead and proposed, and Toni said yes. We went to Lake Havasu near Laughlin, NV, and did the Vegas wedding thing at a local chapel.

Work was going well, and we were growing, exceeding our goals in the first year. Everything was still good at home, but then a friend Toni had gone to school with started coming over with her boy, so he could use the pool. This friend was a drinker, and Toni would drink with her as they hung out by the pool. The friend coming over made me uncomfortable, and Toni's behavior would change when they were together. I'd play with the friend's son in the pool while they would drink. Suddenly, this friend stopped coming over, and I noticed Toni would show up after work with a six-pack of wine coolers. That was different from when I met her. There were other things, such as her saying she was staying late at work to finish but lying to me about it. At the same time, she told her boss she had to leave early because she wasn't feeling well. Slowly, things began subtly changing. About three months into the marriage, things were not going well at home, and my job was demanding more of my time, so I wasn't home much.

When I was out of town for a night or two on business, Toni would return to Scottsdale. She said it was to visit her parents, but the story didn't add up. In reality, she was getting back in with the old group she used to run with, who were major druggies. I later found out that the friend stopped coming over to use the pool because Toni had started getting into her previous drug-induced lifestyle behavior, and the friend did not want her son to be around that environment. When I asked Toni why her friend no longer came around, she gave me an evasive answer. She had begun using again, and I never knew she had even had a drug problem. I also found out that Toni had previously been married to a firefighter, and he had left after she used him up. She was so good at deceiving me and living a double life that I never suspected. There was a sense of embarrassment, too, because I didn't want anyone to find out about Toni and her issues. It was like all my past had come back to haunt me. I had spent time refurbishing the boat I brought back from Las Vegas, and we spent some time on the lake. Suddenly, Toni got into a "lake phase," where she wanted to go to the lake every day and started calling in sick to work so she could go there while I was working. Her behaviors just got stranger and stranger as the hold of Crystal Meth ate her up and totally changed her, both physically and emotionally.

It was surreal, like watching a movie, but I did not blame myself. Once, I was out golfing with some customers, including my friend Kelly, when my phone rang. It was Wells Fargo Bank. Toni was trying to empty my savings account, and I told them not to let her take any money out. Kelly thought I was nuts because I stayed and finished our golf game rather than dropping everything to deal with Toni's craziness. I didn't know what to do. I felt so defeated. Here I was, a recovering alcoholic, and we had bought a new house in North Scottsdale so Toni "could be near her friends." Really, she wanted to be closer to her drug connections. I thought moving closer to her family might be a wake-up call, but instead, it was the turning point of her going downhill. One of her drug friends lived in the house behind us, and strange people associated with her drug usage started coming around. Her best friend told me how bad Toni was and how fast she was going downhill due to Crystal Meth. I even tried getting her into a drug rehab program, but there was no reaching her.

Once, we were at a condo I co-owned in Pinetop, Arizona, and she disappeared after dinner, saying she had to run to the store. I knew it was a lie, and sure enough, she was gone for nearly 24 hours.

I figured she probably went to the casino in the area, hooked up with someone who had money or drugs and made a night of it. I never discussed the incident with my parents, who were visiting us in Pinetop and witnessed the whole thing.

Toni started being around less and less and going downhill. At the same time, I continued going to meetings and building the business at Scully. Eventually, I went to live with Mike Boatman in California, temporarily moving into his spare bedroom. I was so scared and never wanted to live in California, but I had to escape the craziness. Meanwhile, Toni had emptied my bank accounts, taking most of my money through some old checks she found. Once I returned from California, I changed the locks on our Scottsdale house and tried to kick her out, but the cops said I couldn't do that. She also wrote bad checks on the accounts, and I had to deal with that. I filed a restraining order against her, but she broke in and secured the doors in such a way that I couldn't get in. The police came and got her out of the house and took her to jail, but she soon got out while I stayed at a hotel. I was so scared. I put all her stuff at the end of the driveway, called her parents, and told them to come to pick it up. Her mom showed up apologetically, and I helped her load up her car. I had a 9mm gun I had bought and began keeping it on the nightstand while I slept. Several times, people tried to break into the house, and Toni started trying to sweet-talk me to get money. She had spent all of what she had taken on drugs. I filed for divorce, and the judge started awarding Toni stuff, such as a Tahoe 4x4 we owned. It was insanity and brought back many shame issues and embarrassment from being in this situation. After the divorce, she finally went away, and I never found out what happened to Toni, even though I asked around.

After the divorce and my finances in ruins, I knew I couldn't take care of the nice house I owned in Scottsdale, so I sold it and had to start over. The loneliness hit me again as I moved to a one-bedroom apartment in Scottsdale. I was wary of relationships at this point, so I focused on my job and continued dreaming about starting my own business. My mentor, Daryll, bought a condo in Scottsdale, and we spent time together talking about my dream of starting my own trucking company.

Other people may have seen it coming, but the stuff with Toni blindsided me. While going through the divorce, there were very few people to ask about Toni besides the one friend. All she could say was that it was "Toni being Toni." She had a history of getting clean and returning to the old lifestyle. We had only been married for one year when we got divorced.

One of the life lessons I learned was that there is a stigma about someone who has long-term sobriety. People tend to automatically think that someone like me with years of sober living under my belt has their life together, even if that is far from the truth. I was back to having trust issues and only a few friends, but it was time to move on to the next chapter of my life.

16

ALL ON 23 RED

After the time with Toni, I found myself alone again while continuing to work at Scully. I knew deep down there was something more, and I needed to start my own company. I couldn't keep going to work every day for someone else. At the same time, I began having visions of myself at 70 years old, still knocking on doors, trying to find business. Sitting in my apartment alone, I started experiencing overwhelming waves of "Oh my God, is this all there is?" I instinctively knew that working for someone else was making them rich. No one tried to talk me out of my dream taking the leap to start my own business, but I was too scared to tell many others about it.

"What have you got to lose," a friend asked me one day while I was sharing my vision, and suddenly the light bulb went off. He was right. I had no money, so I had nothing to lose.

As I was going through this inner turmoil, I talked with Darryl and told him it was time to start my own company.

"What is your plan?" he asked. "Let me see your business plan."

I had no concrete plan, only ideas floating around in my head.

"You're not ready," Darryl said, adding, "You'll know when you're ready."

Time passed, and I began honing and shaping my ideas and developing a concrete, detailed business plan. Finally, I was ready to see Darryl again. I flew back to North Dakota to see him. Darryl was quite ill by then, and we drove to his cabin on the lake.

"Darryl, I'm ready to do it," I told him, describing my vision, right down to the color of the trucks and the markets I wanted to be in.

"Now, you're ready," he said before giving me some profound advice.

"Tim, you shouldn't be afraid of failing but petrified of succeeding."

I didn't understand those words at the time, but years later, I understood. It was all about responsibility and the details of running the business. I came up with two names of people I trusted and approached them, telling them to analyze my business plan and why it wouldn't work. Both called back and said they thought my idea was great and wanted to partner with me, but I instantly knew one of them would not be a good fit. One of those two people I approached was Paul Truman from Truline. I knew I had nothing with which to launch a company, but he did, so I emailed him.

I had no fear about approaching Paul because I was confident my idea would work, and he had the resources to help make my dream a reality. So, we met, and I pitched my peer-dedicated contract services idea. I would set up my company, Estenson Logistics, where clients would lease the trucks, trailer, driver, and an entire delivery solution from us instead of just leasing trucks. Some truck companies, like Ryder, were already using this approach, but we got in on the idea early, just as others began getting the same idea. During my meeting with Paul at a Phoenix coffee shop, we wrote our initial business plan on the back of a napkin. It included having Paul's dad, Grant, become my 50/50 partner. Paul remembers this vividly:

"Tim called me one day and wanted to know if I was going to be in Arizona anytime in the future," Paul recalled. "Since I had other business there, we agreed to meet at a coffee shop, and I did not have to be sold on his idea. Our business (at Truline) was slow at the time. Some equipment manufacturers were offering incentives to buy trucks, so we sketched out a pricing plan on a napkin to cover all the costs. When I returned home, I told my father, who owned Truline, that Tim's idea was good and something we should try. It also made sense for my dad to be a majority owner, banking on his name and reputation and applying it to the new company.

Right off the bat, Estenson got two trucks, which we loaned to Tim, but to make his idea work, he would need ten trucks," Paul continued. This was February of 1999, and we (Estenson) were losing a bit of money every month, so Tim met with my dad in October, who told him the new idea 'just wasn't working.'" I remember Tim told my dad he would work for free to reduce the amount of overhead. My dad agreed but reminded Tim that he had to get to ten trucks by the end of the year.

Well, by December, Estenson Logistics was still stuck at two trucks, and my dad was ready to pull the plug and bring back the trucks we had loaned Tim, so we had another meeting. Tim asked for three more months, and I convinced my dad to give him an extension through the first quarter of 2000. Because my dad was old school, he wasn't big on new ideas, so I had to do some convincing to get the extension until Tim's company took off."

I was desperate when I pleaded for an extension, using the excuse that some companies were willing to come on board with us after the first of the year but not around the holidays. I knew the idea would work, and I wanted it so badly. But, in my quieter moments, I was nervous and began second-guessing my concept. Truline agreed to pay me $400 weekly for my expenses because I was living off my credit cards. I had nothing to fall back on.

Suddenly, I experienced a life-changing moment. I returned to my room one day, realizing the rent was due, and I had nothing. I was at my wit's end, about to give up, and was emotionally low. I wound up renting a room in a house for $300 a month from the friend of a friend, so at least I had some place to stay. Out of desperation, I went into the casino and indulged in their $1.99 all-you-can-eat breakfast, stuffing myself so I didn't have to eat the rest of the day. As I passed the roulette wheel, I had about $180 in my pocket. On impulse and perhaps out of desperation, I put all my money on "23 red." It hit, and I won more than $6,000. I have no idea why I chose 23, but since then, 23 has been my "lucky" number. The winnings kept me going for a couple more weeks. While I hesitate to call it a "God moment," it was a lifeline that kept me going, let me eat, buy gas, and pay rent, waiting for things to begin breaking my way.

We got through the holidays, and suddenly, things began clicking. Truline and Estenson landed some of Home Depot's business, when another carrier went belly up, and, just like that, we were at ten trucks but had no drivers. We had to scramble to make it work. While we lost money at first, things started breaking for us with our first location in La Mirada, California. Paul's and my strengths were our ability to attract quality people and people who cared. In less than two weeks, we came up with rental trucks, and trailers, staff, and other components that allowed us to start that La Mirada location and become successful.

> "The people were key," Paul added, "and we were able to attract those who could see a larger picture and wanted to be part of something bigger. Every step of the way, we attracted good employees, and the best ones stayed. In addition, having another company

go out of business and us getting the Home Depot contract was huge, because of their reputation and the impact that had on getting other businesses to give us a chance."

"Tim's concept was a good one, forming a partnership with the shippers. If the customer was more efficient, they saved money, but paid for inefficiency, so there was an incentive for them to improve. The hardest part was convincing the customers to buy into the idea, and I don't think Tim realized at the time how hard it would be to break in as a new company. But he was persistent and is still the best salesperson I've ever come across."

"Tim was like Cortez, burning the ships and working 18-hour days to make it happen," Paul recounted. I always kept snacks and a bottle of water with me, because I knew there were times traveling with Tim that we wouldn't take time to stop and eat."

Yes, that's true. Some people didn't want to travel with me because of my relentlessness and drive, at a level some people didn't want to deal with. I remember sometimes we would work all night putting together a PowerPoint presentation, printing it out at Kinko's, and then presenting it to a prospective client. Some people could not handle that kind of schedule, and in the early years, we would be away from home for extended periods.

I remember one new startup we were awarded in Texas. Mike Boatman, our VP of Operations, and I flew there. Remember, we had no business in Texas and only a couple weeks to start a large operation, so we worked 16 to 20 hours daily. After living in a Texas hotel for months, we hired some drivers and had our trucks and trailers in place. We had been at the hotel for so long that the person working at the front desk felt so bad for us that she started doing our laundry in their commercial washer and dryer. We would return to our rooms in this cheap hotel, and our clothes would be folded and laid on our beds.

Soon, the operation was ready to go live, and we were finally breathing again. We had set the number of loads we would ship daily, but on day one, our crew realized they missed their estimates. Moving forward, we would be shipping three times what the initial assessment said. Mike and I looked at each other and said we'd make it happen, and we did. We experienced huge success in that monster distribution center, which helped us grow even faster than we already were. From that point on, we proved we were the shipping company of choice. As a result, our business started growing by more than 100% a year for several years. Oh, and everyone survived.

Our perseverance and drive paid off. Eventually, Paul and I would go to an industry conference where we would feel like the small fish in the big pond. But after listening to the big boys, we would scratch our heads, wondering how they were still in business because they didn't have nearly the organizational structure we had put together. We realized we were better off than we thought we were compared to others in our industry. I remember Paul saying one day:

> "We could talk for days about our different experiences, challenges, and accounts," Paul agreed. "It was a magical journey starting Estenson Logistics. We worked hard and long hours and were blessed. We learned a lot along the way [and] never stopped trying new things, eventually perfecting and improving what we were doing. The lesson for others reading this is that there is still opportunity out there for those willing to put in the work."

I agree with Paul that the American dream is alive and well, and opportunities are still there. Miracles still happen. We can still chase our dreams and build something bigger than ourselves. Paul and I have had and still have a level of respect for each other, along with what we can do collectively and what we can do individually.

Together, we created a foundation utilizing our complementary skill sets and mutual respect.

> Sam Walton used to say, "Walmart was a 30-year overnight sensation," Paul concluded. Some people thought it was the same with us. Many didn't know how much we sacrificed and didn't see the years of sweat and struggle but only saw the finished product. It takes a lot of hard work and commitment to build a successful business.

17

ONCE IN A LIFETIME

I started Estenson Logistics in 1999, after quitting my job at Scully. I had accepted an invitation to a business event in Las Vegas while working at Scully's, but then realized I still wanted to attend under the umbrella of my own company. So, I reached out to Traci, the event coordinator, and told her I wanted to come as a representative for my company. She was not sure she could do that but got the approval after talking with her boss.

> I was coordinating the event in Las Vegas, and Tim told me he had confirmed attending. He said he was transitioning to a different company and wanted to bring a friend. He also asked for an additional golf bag, the premium we were giving away, for his friend. *Who the hell are you?* I thought. *Just a typical sales guy.*
>
> He called me back later, and we were flirting on the phone, and then he phoned a third time because I had told him I had to have the change confirmed with my boss.

Keep in mind, I did not know this woman or anything about her. But I felt comfortable flirting with and teasing her. For example, during one of our calls, I asked her if she would be in Las Vegas.

"Yes, I'm the event coordinator for the golf tournament," she said.

"Oh, are you bringing your husband and family?" I asked.

"No, I'm not married," she told me, "I'll just be coming on my own."

We talked over the next few weeks, and I suggested we get together for dinner since she was traveling alone.

"No, I don't think so because I'll be working," she responded. I think she thought I was being pushy for even asking.

"Well, you think about it," I responded, knowing I had a few weeks to convince her. Traci said she did her own investigation:

> "I didn't know Tim from Adam, so I asked a business associate about him. He went on and on about what a great guy Tim was and said I should treat him well. 'You better not hurt him,' he warned me."

*Hurt **him**, I thought. What about me?*

After our conversation, I did feel more relaxed about meeting Tim, and I started rethinking the dinner invitation, not having any expectations it would lead to anything. Meanwhile, Tim continued calling, and I gave him a lot of crap. He dished it right back, and I remember thinking, *This guy can hold his own.* I was impressed and agreed to meet him for dinner.

Then, Tim had another brilliant idea. "Tell you what," he said, "I'll pick you up at the airport."

"How will I know you?" I asked.

"Oh, you'll know me," he said.

"Fine," I responded, "but I'm keeping my rental car. And don't you think I'm going to have sex with you on this trip. We're not married."

"Traci don't worry about it," Tim responded, "it's Las Vegas. We'll do a drive-through wedding when you get here and a drive-through divorce before you leave!"

So, I let him pick me up at the airport, and I wondered during the flight how I would know who he was. I also had second doubts about doing this but told my friends I had a date, just in case they tried to get ahold of me."

I decided to greet her with a sign that said, "Vegas Wedding Chapel Welcomes Traci." A lot of people gave me weird looks over that sign. And then, after the flight had landed and people were deplaning, I had an OMG moment. *What if she is uglier than hell? What have I gotten myself into?* I thought as I watched several attractive women deplane and walk right past me. Unbeknownst to me, Traci sat in the back of the plane as I eyed every woman who exited, waiting for someone to respond to my sign. Finally, she came down the ramp and saw the sign. It was such a relief when I saw her. She was beautiful, wearing a black biker jacket, and was about 10 years younger than me.

> I didn't know about not sitting in the back of the plane, so I was almost the last one off and spotted his sign right away. It made me laugh, and my first impression was that he was dreamy and hot. I realized I was instantly attracted to him.
>
> "Oh my God, you've got to be kidding me," I said in reaction to his sign when we finally spoke. "I have a real bad habit. I have to go outside and smoke," I added.

> He gave me crap about that, saying something like, "You've got to be kidding, you're a smoker? Don't you know how bad that is for you?
>
> "I don't care what you say," I replied, and went out to smoke as he followed me out the door."

While she wasn't looking, I lit my cigarette and laughed. I snookered her big time. Traci was funny, smart, and sassy, and our flirtation continued. We had no preconceived notions of what would happen, so we were at ease and 100% ourselves.

> *"What does this hot-looking guy see in me*? I wondered, all the while asking myself, *what is wrong with this guy*? Because he seemed too good to be true. Once we actually met in person, there was an instant attraction both physically and emotionally. We felt like we had known each other our whole lives. Still, that weekend was not without challenges, as Tim came down with the flu and was sick much of the time.
>
> Our first date lasted eight days. Once I met Tim, I instantly trusted him and was at peace, which was odd because it wasn't normal for me to be that trusting. It was funny that I fell for Tim since I had vowed to never date anyone with blonde hair because I had been hurt previously by a blonde guy. But then Tim came along. We were both open and honest, even on the first date. He even tried to teach me how to eat with chopsticks, which I failed at miserably. I still can't use them.
>
> I didn't understand that Tim had no money, even though he told me so. Plus, I never dreamt of having kids, only of meeting my own "Prince Charming." So, after our time together in Las Vegas, I drove back to Phoenix with him before returning to Pennsylvania.

That was the start of our crazy relationship, with neither of us having any expectations of anything long-term.

Speaking of expectations, I had no idea I would be moving to Arizona, and my mom did not react well when I told her. Tim and I had only met in March 1999, and here I was only three months later, ready to move to Phoenix to be with him. Before all that happened, all my relatives came and grilled him during one of his visits. No one understood that I wasn't looking for a rich guy. I was looking for an emotional and spiritual connection. That kind of security was more important to me, as I hadn't had that before in previous relationships. Everyone said I was crazy, but one friend told me, "If you don't go, you'll always wonder." She was right.

We saw each other every weekend, even though we had no money. Tim was in Arizona while I was in Pennsylvania. He was able to use his free Southwest Airlines travel vouchers to visit me, and when those ran out, he contacted friends who traveled a lot to scrounge tickets. A lot of bartering took place in doing that, which we kept up for several months.

When it came time for me to decide about moving to Arizona, Tim said, "This kind of certainty comes but once in a lifetime," quoting a famous line from the film Bridges Of Madison County. He was spot on."

During the move, we used credit cards and hired a moving truck to move Traci. Still, I instinctively knew I needed something bigger than a one-bedroom apartment. I knew some real estate people, and we immediately started looking for a house. Somehow, we were able to qualify for a home loan despite having no income and no credit. By the time Traci's stuff arrived, we were in a three-bedroom house, and it's a good thing because she had more stuff than I thought she had, and our small house was immediately full! Once we got her settled here, Traci was going to look for a job in marketing, even though she did not know how to navigate Phoenix. She found a job working for the same company she had worked for in Philadelphia. The pay was okay, and she had good health benefits.

> I had worked in Philadelphia for a General Electric Capital company, so I knew how to drive in a city from the suburbs. But moving to Phoenix was so different. For example, it shocked me that everything was walled in because everything is so open in Pennsylvania. But I loved that for my first Thanksgiving in Phoenix. I wore a tank top and shorts and enjoyed waking up to sunshine every day. It was a big adjustment to make, especially the first year. We never had a grand plan but trusted God to lead us.

18

PT BOAT OR AIRCRAFT CARRIER

By the time I got my first paycheck from Estenson, Traci and I had more than $100,000 in debt. We used Traci's credit cards to travel, move, and survive, because I had initially gotten no new business. In fact, Truline was still paying me $400 a week. Remember, I started my company several months before Traci came into my life, with no customers or business income. I had sold my house, boat, jet skis, and everything to put into the business. I lived in a one-bedroom apartment, drove a leased car, and paid for everything with credit cards. Traci knowingly walked into this because I was completely honest with her about my past and told her everything while she was still in Pennsylvania.

> "Somehow, we got a mortgage for a house, and I had three credit cards. I used to joke with others, telling them that Tim married me for my money! Meeting Tim was like a brand-new beginning for me, and honestly, I didn't know how we would make it. I called my mom every day after I moved and reassured her about my safety. Tim had told me he couldn't have kids, so I went off my birth control and then got pregnant.
>
> Fast forward four years, our son, Max was born. When I told my mom, she said, "Well, you need to get married," so Tim and I began planning that. We

ended up with 30 people coming to our wedding, and I wondered how we would pay for it, as I was still paying back my dad for the debt from my first marriage. He forgave the rest of my $2,000 debt as a wedding gift, which really helped us financially. Even though life was uncertain, Tim has always been a solutions-oriented person, and we just plowed ahead in faith that God had a plan for our lives."

Our daughter, Sami, was born prematurely and spent two weeks in the ICU. After Sami came home, Traci returned to work for a week before we realized it wasn't a good fit because she wanted to be home. We prayed through the situation, saying to God, "Your will be done."

Then, we began looking for a larger home to accommodate our growing family. And, as icing on the cake, our air conditioner went out three days after the warranty expired, and I had no money to get it fixed! So, we took out a loan to replace it, confident that God still controlled our lives and situation.

According to my business plan, I would break even by the end of the first year and begin drawing a salary. During all this chaos, I started drawing a paycheck from Estenson Logistics while Truline stopped paying me. It was a relief for me as I realized everything was all coming together, just as I dreamed it would.

Then, we landed more business in California. Life got crazy as things exploded, and suddenly, I was traveling a lot. After our success working with Home Depot, many people wanted our business, and we had to turn away some clients. We simply did not have the infrastructure in place yet to handle a big influx of business. However, by the end of our first year, we hit our goal and surpassed our five-year plan by year three. Mike Boatman and Cevin Case were there at the beginning as key players in helping Estenson Logistics grow and expand. Mike remembers those days well:

Tim got some business from another company, and I helped him manage it because he needed additional carriers who had trucks. Although he was a young (19-year-old) salesman and working for E.W. Wylie, we began building a relationship, along with the trust and integrity that went with it. As time went on, we worked on multiple projects together before parting ways and then reconnecting five to 10 years later when we began working together at Scully. We worked together for about five years before Tim left to start his own company. Tim would stay with me when he visited California even though I was a competitor because he couldn't afford a hotel. Finally, he had an opportunity to take on the Home Depot business and actually beat me to it! Sometime later, he approached me about joining him as his Home Depot connection was growing. "I'll give you five years," I told him, thinking I was too close to retirement to take on another major venture. Tim is successful because of the people he surrounded himself with, his honesty, integrity, and treating our drivers (the backbone of our business) with respect.

One of the things we did was hook up with Home Depot in Southern California and manage their distribution centers, keeping the other big companies out. Tim also went to Texas to work with Home Depot, and it was a mess. We had 11 trucks and needed 30 from day one. It was such a cluster that we worked 18 hours a day, seven days a week, for at least six months, trying to make it happen and build the needed infrastructure from scratch. All of our "spare time" was spent strategizing at Waffle House. We had no resources in Texas and hired a guy named Scott, who had been a salesman all his life. One night at about 10:30 or 11:00, we were trying to figure things out and found Scott sitting on the lunchroom floor, crying, frustrated over our crazy schedules, and doubting if we could reach our goals. He was completely stressed by the long hours we were putting in and thought we were nuts. Those were tough times, but fun now to look back on. Our philosophy was to get it done, whatever it took. This grew Estenson from nothing to what it became. "Do everything we can to drive down the cost for the customer" was our philosophy and working motto. Through staying in Texas and persevering, we staffed the office with good people and succeeded. As a side note, I also remember that I took a huge pay cut when Tim hired me but have made it back multiple times over the years."

While all this was happening in Southern California and Texas, we bid on a project in Northern California in 2002. That is when Cevin came on board:

I was working with UPS when I answered an ad for this new company. During a subsequent phone conversation, Tim warned me he had a concept in mind, but had not worked out all the details or processes. *How bad could it be?* I wondered.

On Black Friday, I met with Mike Boatman, and the meeting went well. I accepted the job offer, and two weeks later, after leaving UPS, I met Tim for the first time. When we met, all he had was an I-9 and W-4 form for me to sign, and that was my onboarding and company orientation. We went to a meeting with Home Depot almost immediately afterward, and as the Home Depot people were going through their list of projects, Tim kept telling them, "We can handle it." However, the reality was that we had only 40 days to come up with drivers, tractors, staff, and logistics to succeed with this substantial new piece of business.

"Run this like it's your own company to make it work," was Tim's only instruction to us.

Holy Shit," I told my wife, "I think I made a mistake," when I realized how much work had to be done to succeed. But I have to say that Tim and Mike were brutally honest from day one. Tim made customers and drivers the most important elements in building the company. The rest of us were just support staff. All of our success is because of the people. The challenge for me is that I like structure and a plan, while Tim is a free-wheeler, and we were shooting from the hip early on without any structure. *There's no way we can accomplish something like that*, I would think, and my blood pressure would go up. I remember once in Stockton, Mike was putting things together and wrote down the number of trucks we needed and covered it up. When I saw what he had written down, I went ballistic, thinking it was impossible to reach and he was crazy. But somehow, we did it, and often our presentations were better than our multi-milliondollar competitors.

I definitely drank the Kool-Aid and helped the company figure out how to get things done. We had to custom hire at each location for its unique needs. Eventually, we had to build structure, which was my wheelhouse. Tim and Mike got a lot of pleasure in driving me crazy with their free-wheeling style and my need for structure. There were times when I would sit back and think, *there's no f 'ng way this will work*, but time and again, we pulled it off. We never let the customer see the chaos behind the curtain and worked hard, so they only saw the good outcomes and excellent service we were providing. Often, we'd be putting our PowerPoints together late at night, catch a few hours of sleep, then give the presentation the next morning.

> It drove me crazy! But all the insanity brought us together as we spent a lot of time at Mike's house for pizza parties, bonding, and figuring out our 'next steps.'

I have to agree with both Mike and Cevin. We trusted each other and never questioned anything the other person did. In the days before computers, we invented processes and figured out how to make things work. If there was an issue, we knew we couldn't let it go and would deal with it and move on. Each of us had our strengths and weaknesses, and we fed off each other. For example, in hiring, we went after the person with the best personality to match the customers, not necessarily the smartest person. Most of the time in those days, we landed the business we went after, even though we put together presentations at the last minute. All this craziness helped us bond in a way very little else could. We did not want to let each other down. As we grew, it was hard on us because we wanted to be everywhere at once and maintain the "small company" feel. Giving that up was difficult, but I loved knowing these guys had my back no matter what.

About that time, another key person came on board. Michelle Alexander had worked for Circle K and a large electronics company. She answered an ad for an office manager in 2004 and came in for an interview. I don't remember much about bringing Michelle on, as we only spent a few minutes together. Still, she was an immediate asset to our organization, eagerly taking on anything we threw at her. I quickly became comfortable with her and instinctively knew she was a safe person and someone I could totally trust. From running the office to taking on special projects, she has been one of my "go-to" people ever since.

> I had already researched the company and knew some things about them. After working for large corporations, I liked that they were a smaller company. I think I spent about four hours interviewing with multiple people. Then, finally, I met Tim. The vibe was

open, spontaneous, and friendly, not the corporate stuffiness I was used to. I quickly learned that everyone at Estenson wore multiple hats and worked on various tasks, unlike the corporate environment where you "stayed in your lane."

While I had some trepidation about going from a corporate environment to a start-up, I had learned that no job was secure because even large corporations are bought and sold. One thing that impressed me about Estenson Logistics was the relationship between Paul and Tim. Sometimes they would scream and yell at each other, but they always worked things out and put aside personal differences to get the job done.

I was there as the company grew from a handful of people to several thousand spread out in multiple locations. I went from office manager to more of a "corporate manager," with many undefined duties. That included managing payroll, the front desk, HR, and billing. There was initially some overlap, as Truline handled some of the tasks from their Las Vegas offices. But eventually, we moved things like billing and accounts payable to our Phoenix office. As people left the company, I often temporarily inherited their tasks until we brought a new person on board. As we grew, recruiting people to work for us became harder because our insurance coverage wasn't what it should have been for a company our size.

We never made it about money, but more so about treating people fairly. I dressed up when I had to, but I was basically a blue jeans guy at heart. I spoke my mind, and because of that trait, Michelle, at times kept me out of some meetings, especially those dealing with insurance rates, unions, and the like. I have always been logical in my thinking and couldn't understand how insurance companies thought and made their determinations. It just didn't make sense to me, and that fueled some of my anger. Despite the challenges, we never passed those insurance costs on to the customers.

We used to have Christmas parties on the same day in multiple locations, such as Phoenix, Southern California, and Northern California, hopping on a plane to get to the next party. We invited the spouses to participate and become an extended part of our company. Some companies think treating others like crap is okay, and employees are scared to talk because they need their paychecks. One thing that really catapulted us was the idea that we were the PT boat, capable of reacting quickly, rather than the battleship or aircraft carrier that took a long time to turn around. We could respond rapidly without corporate inertia or multiple meetings about how to proceed. We let our people make decisions at the local level, without corporate input, even if our people made a mistake. We made sure we backed them up, correcting them by teaching them a better way down the road.

19

FUNDAMENTAL LEADERSHIP PRINCIPLES

In building a successful, multi-million-dollar business, I have been blessed to have key people like Paul Truman, Mike Boatman, Cevin Case, and Michelle Alexander come along at the right time. Each of them and many others played a crucial part in the success of Estenson Logistics. Early on, we worked on core principles and building blocks that we maintained throughout the company's history as we grew from a startup to a national presence in our industry. Some of the fundamental principles we discovered along the way, in no particular order, were:

1) Discover everyone's strong points and use them to complement each other. For example, Cevin is the "detail guy." He functions best in a structured environment where he knows the plan and sees the course ahead clearly mapped out. On the other hand, Mike and I are more "seat-of-our-pants" individuals and figure things out as we go. While that drove Cevin crazy, it allowed us to say "yes" to opportunities where we didn't see a way forward. As a result, we discovered we could accomplish more than we thought we could.

2) Leveraging Previous Successes. Before joining Estenson, Mike had worked for three other successful startups, all of which had ten or fewer trucks to begin with, so he knew what it took to succeed. Both Cevin and I had gained valuable experience working at other companies as well. Because of this, we were confident we could deliver better customer service at a lower cost than the competition.

Our experience landing Home Depot as a client helped us grow tremendously. Having them as a reference brought great credibility and helped us find the right people to add to our team.

3) Build a culture of respect. The respect Paul, Cevin, Mike, and I had for one another evolved and became the foundation of our company's culture, right down to the people behind the scenes and our drivers. All of them allowed us to grow. "Happy driver, happy customer" was our mantra. Early on, we realized that having great, and committed drivers was the key to our success. "This culture permeated down to the customer, and they embraced it, and we gained their trust and respect," Cevin added. "That meant everyone was on the same page. Mike liked going out with the drivers to let them know they were an important part of the team, which is something few management people do."

4) Think Big, Act Quickly, and Diversify: We figured out early on that there was nothing we couldn't resolve, if we put our heads together. This mindset spread throughout the company, from management down to each employee.

"It was harder for a big company to pivot as quickly and nimbly as we could, as they had too many levels of management. We were the PT boat able to pivot quickly, not the aircraft carrier that took forever to turn," Mike's analogy really stuck with me and I remember him saying further:

> A couple of new customers came along (such as HJ Baker, Home Delivery for Home Depot, and a dairy company) that I (Mike) had to talk Tim into. A huge step was when the dairy business wanted us to take over much of their operation, with a lot of cash and resources. That was a great leap of faith for us.

Another lesson we learned when Home Depot comprised 90 percent of our business was that it was not healthy for us to have most of our eggs in one basket. Therefore, we went after other clients, eventually making Home Depot about half our overall business.

5) Disagree Without Becoming Disagreeable. We had disagreements and issues with several operations where the customer wanted the impossible. We were all smiles to the customer but may have said, "oh shit," among ourselves and argued over the details of how to make it happen. There was always give and take in such situations where we disagreed. Still, we took ideas from everyone on our team as we battled to make things happen. As Cevin said:

> We had disagreements at times, but it wasn't really arguing, just figuring things out. Sometimes, certain departments didn't want to row in the same direction, and our 'discussions' got heated, but eventually, we worked it out. We could argue and be pissy with each other, then go out for a beer and work it out. That's how tight the bond between us was. We were able to move beyond the petty stuff, always remembering that the customer came first. The respect and camaraderie among the team members drove us to work together toward the best solution.

6) Celebrate the Victories. Our personalities were such that we would charge the hill, conquer it, and look for the next challenge without looking back at our accomplishments. That was a mistake in retrospect, but at the time, we were moving ahead too fast to look in the rear-view mirror. As we grew, celebrating those accomplishments became harder, but Mike tried, with some success, to get us to do that. If I had to do it differently, I would take time to celebrate the team and each accomplishment along the way. It wasn't a big deal for us to get an award, as it was expected. We did accept accolades from customers, such as Home Depot, who were then the nation's second-largest retailer. Getting an award from them was a huge deal, and they would use us as an example to some of our competitors. We won their coveted "Partner of the Year" award several times. I was most gratified by them pointing to us as an example for other companies to emulate.

> I enjoyed going to these large gatherings and having the big guys come up to us and ask how we did it. It made me so proud to be in that situation. We were doing things the way the big carriers weren't able to do," Cevin remembered.

7) Learn From Your Mistakes: We made mistakes and tried to initiate changes to make things better. For example, our company policies resulted from things that went wrong, such as a disgruntled employee who sued us. However, we learned and built a more stable company from those mistakes, and it was humbling to watch the growth as we applied the necessary changes. For example, if our dispatcher had drivers in remote locations and we had no backup, we would fly a driver in or train someone from another company as needed.

> We even trained dispatchers to drive for us, all to provide the best possible service for the customer and get the job done," Mike added. "Prime Source was another case where we didn't have the resources to meet the customer's needs but figured it out. Tim let us make those decisions and always backed us up. So, you didn't want to let the team down, but at the same time you weren't so afraid of making a mistake. Tim empowered us to make decisions and always backed us up. If you made a mistake, you cleaned it up but were never reprimanded for it."

8) Commit to Customer Service. We would do whatever it took to get the job done for the customer, which became more costly as we got bigger. We put pressure on ourselves and didn't want to let each other (and the team) down. If someone was struggling, we would go to them and offer them help to strengthen the company, which was different from how things worked in other larger companies. We were all frustrated when we got to be such a big company that we lost that personal touch.

20

KNOW WHEN TO HOLD 'EM & WHEN TO FOLD 'EM

Every year, beginning in about 2000, the driver shortage grew as a large portion of that population began retiring. In addition, the up-and-coming younger generation did not want to become truck drivers. Construction workers made more money and got to be home every night rather than be on the road all week. The rigors of travel and being on the road constantly made trucking less attractive to the generation raised on electronic devices. This became a challenge for us as we continued growing with more locations.

Mike was the first to get out because, as he put it, "I quit having fun because we had gotten so big as a company. It wasn't the company we had started, and the levels of bureaucracy had gotten bigger. So, I was ready to back away and retire again."

> "When we were at 600 to 700 trucks and got in with the dairy company and larger fleets, we diversified so much, especially geographically, that it became more difficult to manage. When we were smaller, every department was involved in a new startup. As we grew, we lost that, and it became frustrating. We weren't able to keep that small company feel. That's when I began feeling it. We were forced to grow for the sake of the company, but that complicated the problem," Cevin added.

I had come to the same conclusion and the loss of that small-company feel, led me to a monumental decision. I had to sell the company.

Mike retired in 2012, which came as no surprise. The joke for years had been that he was on a "rotating retirement plan." Mike had great relationships with the customers, who knew they could always call him if there was a problem, and he would fix it. We were in 28 states and nearly 98 operating locations, many in California. With all the success Mike had achieved, he always moved on before companies reached a certain size. He was the number two guy in our company, and it got to the point where the company outgrew Mike. It just wasn't fun for him anymore because, as a business, we had become so compartmentalized that we had lost that small company feel and couldn't react as quickly as we used to. We had lost the "Estenson Way," the very hands-on blueprint of how we began and operated. It was frustrating for him, and he was ready to retire.

We had been grooming Cevin to take over Mike's role as vice president of operations and COO. He easily moved into that role. At the same time, we added multiple people under Cevin because we were growing so fast. No one wanted to fail the customer or me. The good news was that the customer did not notice any difference with our upper management changes because our site managers were empowered to make decisions. Even if they were wrong, we would back them up and fix things internally. We did a good job transitioning from Mike to Cevin despite their different management styles, making it seamless for the customer. That's what matters most.

Our plan worked on another level as well. The average driver turnover in large companies is more than 100% per year, but for us, it was about 27%, which was also reflected in customer retention. Our renewal average for retaining clients in the 20-year history of Estenson Logistics was more than 98%. In contrast, the industry average was 60 to 65 % based on the typical three-to-five-year contract. As a result, we grew from about $200 million a year in sales to roughly $360 million in those five years. Despite our tremendous success, I knew I had to sell and made an agreement to do so in May of 2017. During that transition, I appointed myself the direct contact with Home Depot since they were our largest customer. Michelle remembers those days:

> When I started, we had about 250 employees. Eventually, the company grew to more than 3,000, and I saw the writing on the wall. I felt bad for Tim because he carried the burden for all these families and all the other stuff going on, such as lawsuits and other legal challenges. Rumors were constantly swirling about the company being sold, and everyone always wound up venting in my office. I always told people the truth, even to those who didn't want to hear it and wouldn't put up with people just coming to me to bitch and moan without proposing a solution. It wasn't until Paul took me aside and told me we needed specific documents regarding a possible sale that I began taking the rumors seriously. But I knew I would land on my feet somewhere if Estenson Logistics got sold.
>
> On the other hand, I thought that things would be different with the bigger company taking over. Maybe the benefits would be better, especially the 401(k), because I was one who saved a lot of my income. I tried to put a positive spin on things, and initially, things were okay under the new owners. Eventually, the new company began micro-managing our division without telling us. We were being left out of the loop, but I decided to ride it out as long as I could. The hardest thing for me was losing the ability to protect my department and the people to whom I was closest. The management style was totally corporate, unlike what we had developed at Estenson. I lasted a little over a year under the new owners. In fact, the day I gave my notice, another HR person did the same. The new company showed its

true colors as other people left when I did or shortly after. Very soon, there were no Estenson people left at the new company. Meanwhile, Tim used to tell me, "When you're finished with this, I've got something else," but I never took him seriously, thinking he was just trying to make me feel better. Little did I know I would eventually return to work for him after he left the company a while after I did.

Despite our success and growth, we typically dealt with 10 to 20 lawsuits at once, primarily frivolous in nature. I was sick and tired of being sick and tired. But I kept going because I felt I owed it to the employees, but eventually, I couldn't do it anymore. We gave employees generous pay and benefits while I looked for a company that needed the people we had. I found a publicly traded company, not in the transportation business the way we were, but hired independents to deliver their goods. They were a non-asset-based company, and their customers began pressuring them to consolidate their operations into a "one-stop-shop." Hence, they determined they had to buy a specialized trucking company. That made us attractive to them. They needed all our people, expertise, and equipment, so I was comfortable that my employees wouldn't be laid off when I sold. Through negotiations, I ensured they kept some of our leadership and negotiated a pool of money and stock options to be distributed to key employees. As a result, many of our employees got significant payouts, kept their jobs, and got raises and stock options. Several got enough of a payout to pay off their homes. These deals usually take several years to finalize, but the new company put a definite date on the close of the sale, which was extremely rare in our industry. That worked well for us as leverage. On June 31, 2017, we closed on the sale of Estenson Logistics. Cevin stayed with the new owner as their operations manager until 2020.

Looking back, I wish I had sold the company two to three years earlier, as the road to mentally and emotionally letting my company go was difficult. I was ready, tired, and burned out from how hard I pushed myself. It had taken a toll on me, leading to internal struggles battling my home life, its issues, and the business stuff. Through all of this, I went to meetings steadfastly and reminded myself that I was where I was because of my sobriety. "But for the grace of God, there go I." The meetings kept me anchored and realizing, "Yes, I am an alcoholic." But I never celebrated my business accomplishments and victories because I felt undeserving. It was the shame and fear of failure talking.

The new owners did everything they promised, and I stayed on for one year, but it wasn't pretty at the end. I had worked with the man who started the company and had two sons working there. The gentleman I was working with backed out of the operation at the age of 72, and I never clicked with the son. He started making horrible management decisions that I disagreed with. It was miserable for me and hard on some of our employees. It was hard to walk away emotionally, but I was ready to be done when the company changed hands. However, I got excited to stay on because they had contacts who wouldn't talk to Estenson Logistics because we weren't big enough. Suddenly, we had access to large companies, such as Target, Lowes, and Dollar General. The problem was these large companies wanted us to do things cheaply, which I didn't want to do for just one or two percent return.

After I left, the new company began losing business and making demands on clients. This fueled my frustration because the son wanted to raise rates drastically on some existing clients while "giving away" our services to these big companies. The new management didn't understand why they shouldn't raise rates on existing customers. It was a frustrating time, and many of my former employees got fired as I was leaving, adding to my frustration. That included axing experienced employees to cut costs, while was demanding rate increases as significant as 18%. The mindset was partly ego-driven by the new management, who wanted the prestige of boasting about working with large, well-known companies while jacking up the rates with existing customers. Overall, it was a frustrating time of transition for me. I was ready for a new challenge but knew I needed a go-to person to get things organized. Of course, I immediately thought of Michelle.

> In the summer of 2018, my husband and I were heading to Costa Rica, and when we landed, my phone blew up. Tim and Traci were texting me about this new opportunity they dangled before me. When I returned home, I agreed to go to work for Tim again.

Traci and I knew that Michelle was the right fit for us to help manage both our personal and business interests. Not even in my wildest dreams, could I have known that I would eventually be building a racing team or doing some of the fun things I did next. Through it all, Michelle helped us keep all of it organized. Traci saw it before I did and was enthusiastic about bringing Michelle on board. When Michelle began working for us, the joke was that the job description would come in time. In other words, there was no initial job description or specific tasks because they morphed as we grew. For example, that's how the racing team evolved. Traci and I had a lot of things that needed to be done, and with Michelle on board, we knew they would get done. For example, when we decided to buy a semi for our racing team, Michelle made all that happen, cutting through all the paperwork and red tape to make it happen. Through it all, we tried to have fun at work and not let the stress get to us.

> It was so slow at the beginning, but I utilized that time to prepare us for when things got busier, so we weren't caught off guard. Eventually, my job entailed everything from paperwork to buying a new truck to designing and ordering T-shirts for our racing team. I never knew when Tim walked through the door what new project he would throw my way. But I was always up for new challenges. It has been such a ride for me from the first time I interviewed at Estenson Logistics until today. I remember one funny story from my time at Estenson Logistics. We had one employee

who was consistently and chronically late for work. Then, one day, she called in late, but this time, she had the most creative (and legitimate) excuse I had ever heard: She forgot to charge her "electric, artificial leg!" Best. Excuse. Ever!

Pseudonym chosen for anonymity*

21

"RETIREMENT"

After selling the company and staying on for a year, I "retired" on December 31, 2018, but retained an ownership stake in Truline Corporation. However, I was bound by a non-compete clause that ended on July 1, 2020. During this timeframe, I did not have anything to do with Truline. Still, I needed something to do.

I was in the hospital after undergoing the first of two hip replacements when Traci told me I needed a hobby and something to do. She was nervous about me going into retirement and hanging around with nothing to do, especially since our kids were almost grown.

> My first reaction was I didn't want to spend all my time at home with Tim, and we both knew he needed something to do to keep him motivated and involved. I knew he would drive me nuts otherwise and interrupt my routine because we had never spent much time together since he was always traveling.

So, I decided to return to my roots: motorcycle racing and collecting vintage motorcycles. Soon, my collection went from two to 20 to 50 to hundreds. At its peak, I owned about 350 motorcycles. Today, I'm at about 310. This was the beginning of Estenson Racing, born out of my passion for motorcycles and flat-track racing and came soon after I began collecting bikes. Traci reminded me there is more to life than just working. She helped me to realize my dream when we decided to help one rider in particular, Colt Chebultz. He rode with us for about 18 months, which eventually led to us adding another racer and expanding to an entire team. We were doing well racing and having fun. Still, I was constantly watching other riders and looking for up-and-comers and other potential team members, such as "Haulers," who helped us get from race to race.

We would drive around first in a Mercedes Sprinter van and then in a hauler truck, which included a shop in the back and sleeping quarters. At the same time, we separated from Colt and brought Sammy Halbert on board, and I also hired a crew chief, Teddy McDermott. All of this was to make us more competitive. We also switched to Yamaha motorcycles, modified one of our bikes from 60 HP to more than 100 HP, and gradually improved our racing performance. We usually finished in the top ten and sometimes in the top five. As things continued to evolve, I decided we should have a single-class rider and found Dalton Gauthier. I signed him to run as a separate part of our team. He did really well in the first four races we entered. Then, unfortunately, he had some personal problems and eventually left our team.

Meanwhile, we struggled to build the best bike possible and continued to look for new riders. Then, the McDermotts left, and I decided to move everything in-house. That is when we began our shop and workplace locally in Arizona. Mike Boatman returned for a while as one of my drivers, and as the years went on, riders came and went. Kolby Carlisle came on board in 2017, the same year we won the singles championship, which was almost unheard for your first year with a new rider. The following year, Kolby raced again for me, and we continued hiring team members. Today, we have 22 team members. And, that's after starting with just three. The passion for racing reignited inside of me. I wanted to give our riders the support I never received when I was racing, wanting them to accomplish what I never could. Seeing them compete brought back the passion from when I raced, although that seemed like another lifetime ago.

"I'm living through you," I told our riders, reminding them I wasn't talented enough and didn't have the same equipment available to them that they do today.

When we show up at races, we are the most professional-looking and best factory-supported team out there. That's the way I want it. Today, we are a state-of-the-art team, consistently finishing among the top teams in the country. Our latest rider, Dallas Daniels, came on board in 2020 and won the singles championship. He also returned to win the same championship in 2021, which had never been done before. After moving up in class, he also won Rookie of the Year in 2022. "Driving for excellence, driving to win, and building a team" is our motto and what I'm all about.

Meanwhile, I spent the next few months playing with the motorcycle collection and building the racing team, continuing to grow it. Our "office" and motorcycle collection were in an airplane hangar, which I thought I would never fill up. However, Traci instinctively knew better, telling me it was not big enough. She was right as I filled the rest of the building with our racing equipment.

As the team grew, we needed a new shop and workplace. This led to me buying a building with offices at the Chandler, Arizona, Airpark. At the same time, I met a guy who also owned part of the building, and we started talking. I told him I was going to collect motorcycles and pursue motorcycle flat-track racing. He owned four adjacent hangers, and after we spoke, I bought all four of them. While it was a lot of work, it was also stuff I love doing, so it felt like something other than work. I set up a machine shop so we could build our own parts and frames, and Yamaha even stepped in as a sponsor for our team. Traci knew retirement for me was not sitting around doing nothing. So, she wasn't surprised that I built the Estenson Racing Team and expanded my motorcycle collection. My philosophy is simple: Everything in the economy is cyclical; part of success is knowing where you are in that cycle. I am considered "Aggressively conservative" and usually won't plunge into things unless I see I can make a profit and minimize my risk.

Next up, we bought a 10,000-square-foot shop and warehouse and then added on. We also bought a condo complex next door and four more airplane hangars, one of which is a machine shop. That makes six airplane hangars. The condo complex houses riders when they come to Phoenix for training during the winter back East. We also set them up at a facility for physical training and provided nutrition coaching for the riders. Most of the team lived in the Midwest and had grown to a point where we needed to open a second race shop. We chose Owensboro, Kentucky, because most of our races are in the Midwest and East. We're also on airport property in Owensboro, so my "office" there is about 50 yards off the runway!

During this time, Traci began getting involved with a lot of philanthropic work, which she excelled at, working as hard as I did in building my business. We also used some of the hangar space for her activities. She tells it best:

> I had always been big with the Parent Teacher Organization (PTO) and teacher's appreciation groups, and someone asked me to be a part of The East Valley Women's League, which I joined. They had about seven different charities, and everyone had to work the Cinderella Affair. A year later, I chaired the same event.
>
> The Cinderella Affair is an all-volunteer project supported by the East Valley Women's League. Our mission is to make attending prom affordable for all high school juniors and seniors in Arizona and make it an event in their lives to remember! The program was founded in 2002 to assist girls by collecting and distributing new and gently used formalwear. At one point, we gave away more than 2,000 dresses, shoes, and jewelry to high school-age girls. As a result, we've had as many as 1,200 girls wait in line to get dresses and accessories. The Cinderella Affair has

also provided dresses for exchange students from the Tempe Sister Cities program.

We turned one of Tim's buildings into a Cinderella's Castle, complete with a meeting room. The Pregnancy Care Center was also something I decided to help out with, and I ended up getting involved in other organizations helping with clothing and other needs. We're also involved with special needs kids at Christmas and have parties and special events. I didn't want to miss the opportunity to help others, especially local youth groups and those in need. My involvement inspired Tim to get on board with the charity arm of his racing world.

"Rookies of 79" is a charity created by six motorcycle racers who were ending their careers. They took their original $600 to form the charity that helps injured flat-track motorcycle racers via a 501 (c) 3. They help professional and amateur racers with out-of-pocket medical costs and cover funeral costs for those who die because many riders can't get health and life insurance due to the dangers of racing. I helped organize the charity, ensured it was set up properly as a 501(c) 3, and assisted with bringing in corporations to support it. Nowadays, it is sustainable as a genuine charity and has generated more than three million dollars to help countless riders and their families.

In 2018, I started a company with Pat Farley called Enso Discoveries and Enso Doctors, centered around platelet-rich plasma (PRP) and platelet-rich fibrin (PRF). The products are designed to significantly enhance animals' lives by developing relevant, cost-effective, novel technologies to assist veterinarians in their work. The company is also expanding its research to provide products for humans.

I'm also involved in a charity called Shots for Soldiers. They help cut through the bureaucratic red tape and partner with decision-making physicians who believe serving this country matters and are willing to help those who served. From this, we can provide potential pain relief using Enso Doctors Rebound PRP services to Veterans who cannot normally afford it or do not know about this service. In addition, we donate products to help veterans.

Unfortunately, COVID slowed the growth of these endeavors for two years. During that time, we did a lot of research and development. Still, we were able to keep all of our staff on during Covid to continue research. These products developed by Enso work for pain, sleep, and anxiety. Some of them contain THC, while others do not. We manage the product from the growing fields through harvest, processing, and production. I got into this during the last few years I was working when I began experiencing a lot of pain from age and stress. My doctors realized I was blocking out the pain, but eventually, it caught up to me. I teamed up with Pat Farley, who started a stem-cell business, Kansas Regenerative Medicine, and began getting stem-cell shots. But for me, it would take a long time to take effect, and I thought it wasn't working. Then, suddenly, it would work. As I talked with him, we devised the PRP process, which I tried. Pat saw a niche for this, and we began working together as partners. That led to the founding of Enso Discoveries and product creation during the two years of Covid.

Today, for the most part, I'm a minority owner of Truline, but I have stayed as a quiet partner and haven't gotten involved in the daily rat race, which is fine by me. However, we have brought back a few key people from the Estenson days. Cevin is back on the dedicated contract side with the goal of growing that aspect of the company. Nikki Rodgers came back, is in charge of analytics and pricing, and works with the finances. I got involved in trying to bring in past customers and have helped the company grow again by landing some old clients from the Estenson days, such as Home Depot, Nestle, and Kroger.

These days, I'm involved with the Estenson Vintage (Motorcycle) Collection, Estenson Racing, Truline, and Enso Discoveries (with its subsidiaries). My traveling these days is mainly centered around racing, but occasionally, my other business ventures also require some travel. The racing schedule includes every weekend in the fall and some in the spring. The beauty of it is Traci and I spend a lot of time together and share some of these adventures. Our day typically begins slowly, with coffee together and spending time talking before starting our day. I must say, I am truly grateful for this time together and this stage in our lives!

22

THE SPIRITUAL JOURNEY

Throughout this book, I've touched upon the spiritual path of my life in recovery, which remains an important part of who I am today. Unfortunately, I received little in the way of spiritual input as a child. In about fourth grade, Mark, Marcia, and I were sent to church, but my dad wouldn't attend because his drinking was out of control. My parents decided to drop us off at Sunday School at an area Lutheran church, thinking we needed some spiritual input.

Our Lutheran background was partly cultural because there are many Lutherans in North Dakota and the Midwest. I became resentful about being forced to attend and viewed it as a punishment, mostly because I saw Sunday as my free time away from school to do what I pleased. Attending church or Sunday School cut into that free time and fueled the resentment toward my mom. It was difficult for me to sit quietly in church or Sunday School. I existed in an ongoing state of anxiety, but not to the extreme of suffering from panic attacks. But back then, my condition went undiagnosed, and I just lived with it. My anxiety wasn't necessarily a reaction to church but my way of coping with people and new situations. A lot of it came from not doing well in school and having poor reading skills, which fed into my low self-esteem.

As far as what I learned in the church setting, I had no reaction to the words or concepts of God. *Why the hell did we need to know about God?* I wondered because he was irrelevant in my life. Initially, my mom took us to church and Sunday School, but we made such a fuss that eventually, the compromise we agreed to was for us to only have to go to Sunday School and not the church service.

I thought of most of my time spent at church as 'putting in my time'. I was ready to get out of there. They spoke about God making everything better, but I didn't believe it. It made no sense to me at a young age. *If there was a God, I'm not in His life, and He isn't in mine*, I thought at the time. By the time I reached eighth or ninth grade, my concept of God changed to Him being a punishing God. There was no concept of God as a loving father because that was way over my head. That teaching only fueled my anger because of the fact that I had to be there, but my dad didn't. It was also about that time when I started getting in trouble, feeding into my concept of God as a punishing being.

As my dad entered an inpatient treatment center and my mom began Al-Anon, they began learning more about God but didn't force their new-found beliefs on me. However, I did rebel against the teachings from recovery that my parents were getting, as my drinking and wild behavior began surfacing, leading me to hate and resent God even more. Also, being exposed to God at the few Alateen meetings I attended around age 16 fueled my resentment. The people there talked about God and spiritual things in recovery, but it just made me angrier. When they spoke of "the alcoholic" in the meetings, I thought they were talking about me, pushing me further away from God or any higher power. It felt forced.

Ironically, it was the same Lutheran church I had to attend as a child, as it was later for my sister's wedding and that three day bachelor's party I mentioned earlier. The one where I had to leave the ceremony to go throw up...Yeah, not so good memories.

Spiritually, I drifted aimlessly until I entered into recovery. I did pray the "foxhole" prayer when things got bad, as in, "God, get me out of this, and I'll (fill in the blank)." But as with many people, as soon as the problem lifted, God was no longer in my thoughts. Throughout it all, I never called myself an atheist but said I was agnostic. I think I recognized the vague concept of "a" God, but I never knew what I believed.

One of my spiritual turning points came when I hit rock bottom with my alcohol addiction. I knew my choices in life were to ask my mom for help or kill myself. I entered the treatment program I referenced earlier and began attending meetings and hearing about God. However, it spun me out of control because I didn't understand the whole concept. "I can't do this," I told my mom once, "because I don't understand what they're talking about." As I went through my in-treatment program, I started reading from the AA Big Book. Still, I cringed when I encountered a reference to God and rebelled against the "God" concept. While I had removed alcohol from my life, I hadn't found anything to replace it, which in the recovery world is reliance upon a higher power as a path to sobriety. Slowly, very slowly, as my sobriety grew, I began working the Twelve Steps, skipping Step Three, which is "making a decision to turn our will and our lives over to the care of God as we understood Him." I also glossed over other steps in the program that mentioned God.

But as I began living in sobriety and developing relationships, the guys I hung out with began teaching each other, and funny things started happening. I began seeing miracles happen among the group members as marriages were restored, people found jobs and began turning their lives around. Slowly, I began to understand the concept of God "as you understand him." I started believing in "something out there" but didn't call it "God" as someone who controlled my life and destiny. I recoiled at the very idea of that kind of control. Yet, ironically, that is precisely what my addiction had done for many years.

Remember earlier, when I said I noticed that painting of Jesus guiding and pointing the way, while I was speaking at a meeting? Seeing that and having that epiphany changed my life so much that I tore up my notes and talked about that in my presentation, embracing the concept of a spiritual guide directing my path and guiding me in the way I should go. (Psalm 143:8-10)

From there, I was scheduled to work on my Third Step with my sponsor, so without my knowledge, he arranged for me to meet with a pastor in Moorhead, Minnesota. That was the time I drove there while deep in thought, not intending to do so. That day, I was able to turn my will and life over to God as I understood Him. That was a huge step for me, spiritually. Today, I don't view myself as a religious person but as a spiritual one. "Allow me to serve others and not myself" is my daily prayer. Looking back, I went from not understanding anything about God to being resentful of Him, to accepting a higher power as something out there, to truly believing in God and having that faith grow to where He is everything to me.

Today, God is my absolute best friend and someone I can always count on. God and His grace are the only reason I am still alive. It's been quite a spiritual journey, and I look at all of my past adversity as something that has helped me get to where I am today and also given me the ability to help others. My spiritual life is not confined by Christianity, Islam, or any other religious system, and I have never had that point of origin or sought to get it. While I can't think of any particular sacred writings that have impacted me, I read daily meditation books as part of my recovery. In addition, I've learned so much from other people as a "hands-on learner." Despite lacking a traditional religious experience, I have an uncanny spiritual relationship with the God of my understanding. God and my sobriety are my top priority, followed by Traci and then my family.

God promises to let us reenter society on its own terms and not just live (or hide) in AA. That was another awakening for me, learning that it was okay to have a life and friends outside of AA. So many people have a huge fear of leaving their AA comfort zone and become so tied to that that the fear of leaving can be overwhelming. In fact, when I return home to North Dakota and attend a meeting, some of the same people are still there. So often, as recovering alcoholics, we must step out on faith without understanding our decisions, knowing it may be years later until we see the "why."

While we don't go to church very often, when we do, we attend a non-denominational church in the Phoenix area. Even though it is an evangelical church, I still struggle with some concepts they teach, so my approach is to take what I need and leave the rest, which I learned from my sponsor. Today, I do my daily readings and realize eventually, I need to get to a point in my life where going to church and connecting with those delivering the message, and the message itself is more important in my life and recovery. In the meantime, Traci and I are confident and comfortable in our beliefs and living by faith.

23

LOOKING BACK

In writing this book, I realized we would complete the book with Chapter 22. I quickly told Dave, "We have to have a Chapter 23" because 23 has always been my lucky number. If you'll remember, I was in Las Vegas, at the end of my rope, broke, at my wit's end, and trying to start my company. I was exhausted emotionally, physically, and discouraged that my dream seemed to be dead. I walked through the casino to take advantage of their $1.99 breakfast. Afterward, I took the money I had left (less than $200) and put it - for no particular reason - on number 23, red at the roulette wheel. I didn't even wait for the wheel to stop before I walked away, shuffling out with my head down. Suddenly, the dealer hollered.

"23, straight up red, winner!"

I won. I won on 23!

I turned around and picked up my winnings of about $5,700, which was a turning point, allowing me to keep Estenson Logistics going for another 30 days. That windfall let me pay the rent and catch up on maxed-out credit cards and other debts. It is a Hollywood-type story, hard to believe, but true.

I've come a long way from sitting on that windowsill, drugged and drunk, holding a loaded revolver, with my finger on the trigger, and paranoid that people were coming to get me.

At age 15, 16, or even 18, no one would have tagged me as "most likely to succeed." They would have written me off as a hopeless drunk and stoner who would never amount to anything. But, by the grace of God, my life got turned around, and I've been blessed with success and great chances to help others. Recently, I returned to Rapid City, South Dakota, and a surprising number of people I knew from my past showed up. Some hadn't seen me since I was 17 and deep in my addiction. They were amazed at my success and shocked at how far I had come. Many had followed the success of Estenson Racing and were still involved in following the sport. But, of course, with the advent of the Internet, they could Google my name and find out what I had been up to over the past few years. Many saw me as the prodigal child who had come home, and they were genuinely happy for me.

I've lost track of many people who've made some sort of an impression on my life, but a few that I can remember are Rick, who was there after my windowsill experience, was one of those. I never saw him again after leaving my crappy staircase "apartment" in Iowa. The motorcycle shop in Iowa – where I rarely showed up for work while living with my sister and her boyfriend Jay – is still there, although Mo has passed away. Speaking of Jay, he is still in Fargo, where he owns a snowmobile repair shop. His son is a crew chief for a professional snowmobile race team. My sister's ex-boyfriend, Mike, was killed in a motorcycle race while he was living with Marcia. He was in his last year of racing before planning to attend college when he died.

My former party buddy Larry, the last friend I had before getting into recovery, still lives in Sioux Falls, South Dakota, and has survived cancer. We lost touch and grew apart once I left South Dakota, got sober, and went down a different path in life. I lost track of my other party buddies, Harold and Marty after the farm party in Harold's hometown. I never saw either of them again after my last party.

My friend and first AA sponsor, Bud M. (whom you met in Chapter 8), got cancer and passed away in his early 70s. He smoked cigarettes and drank a lot of coffee, leading to his health issues. When I was in my mid-20s, I would pick him up, carry him to my car, and drive him to his doctor's appointments. When he was healthy, we laughed and golfed together, and it was tough for me to watch him waste away and die.

People have asked me about St. John's, where I first got into rehab. I returned there early in my recovery to check in and say hi to those I knew, but eventually, the hospital sold out to a larger group. Sadly, the addiction center there closed as well. Gino, who walked me through recovery after I left St. John's, stayed in my life for several years until I left Fargo. He continued living in AA, going to meetings, and maintaining his sobriety. He had more than 30 years of sobriety when he passed away.

My first real boss, Bob. L, whom I met at an AA meeting in Morehead, continued working at E.W. Wiley Corp. long after I left. Once he retired, his boys took over the company and sold off the trucking division. He took a chance on me when no one else would, hiring me to wash trucks in Fargo during the winter when it was 20 degrees below zero. He passed away about 15 years ago.

Another person from my past, my ex-roommate Mike, left Fargo and moved about 40 miles away to Detroit Lakes, Minnesota. The last I heard, he was a drug and alcohol counselor.

My good friend and mentor, Daryl, stayed in Fargo and would visit me in Phoenix, where he had a condo. Remember, it was my many conversations with Daryl that ultimately motivated me to start my own business. The conversation that really motivated me to formulate my plans to start my own company. He passed away a few weeks after I took his sage advice to launch my business plan and go out on my own. His sage advice was, "Don't spend one minute worrying about failure, but be scared of success." I didn't get it then, but I eventually knew exactly what he meant.

Remember my friend Carl, who moved to Las Vegas with me? He eventually stopped doing business in Las Vegas and moved back to Fargo with his wife and kids. He opened his own electrical contracting business in Fargo doing and is still doing so, as far as I know. We stayed in touch for a while, but not recently.

Paul Truman is still actively involved with Truline (in which I still have partial ownership), and we talk frequently. He still lives in Las Vegas, where his company is headquartered, and continues to be active in the business, as a consultant. Grant Truman passed away about five years ago, but not before turning over his portion of Truline to Paul, who became the company president. Another friend, Cevin Case, is back working full-time as Truline's director of operations, which he took on beginning in 2020.

My friend, Jim, who helped me settle in Phoenix, is still a good friend, and we regularly keep in touch. He and I go way back as someone I met during my early days in AA in Fargo. He still lives and runs his own business in the Phoenix area.

Another good friend, Mike Boatman, lives in Lake Havasu, Arizona, after retiring from Estenson Logistics. He drove the semis for my racing team for a couple of years before stepping down to fully enjoy his retirement.

Michelle Alexander is still working for me at our Chandler, Arizona office, but isn't involved in the transportation aspect of things. She takes care of everything involved with Estenson Racing, my motorcycle collection, and personal business for Traci and me. With her husband's recent retirement, she is assessing her next steps while working several days a week. Apart from work, she loves being a grandma to several kids and enjoying that aspect of life.

Estenson Racing has been a huge part of my life since its inception, and several riders who were instrumental in the team's beginning have since moved on. My first rider, Colt Chebultz, is married, has two children, and has taken over his grandfather's business. He hasn't raced in several years. My second rider, Kolby Carlisle, isn't riding with our team anymore. He has moved to Illinois, where he is still actively racing. He is also a full-time college student pursuing a bachelor's degree.

Outside of racing, I now own 100% of Enso Discoveries, relocated it to Arizona, and continue working to make it more profitable. I am also on the board of directors for Back on Track Racers Recovery, where Ronnie Jones is the director. We work on helping injured racers, or those killed, and their families. It's a way of giving back to injured riders and their families.

As far as family goes, Traci's father has passed away, but her mom, Bertha, is 93, lives in Pennsylvania, and spends about half the year with us in Arizona. I have the best and most fun relationship with my mother-in-law that anyone could ever ask for. With all her grandkids grown and gone out of the house, she spends a lot of time with us.

My dad passed away in 2004, while on one of my company deep-sea fishing trips in Mexico. My mom passed in 2023 from Alzheimer's.

My sister Marcia is doing wonderfully. After selling a sleep clinic business that she was part owner in, she stayed and helped the employees for a year or two and is still involved in it. Retired, she and her now husband Ken moved to Grand Forks, North Dakota, and built a home there. Their only child lives nearby, with Marcia's two grandkids, whom she helps care for. Although retired, Ken works with our race team at every event as a "fly-in guy," coming into town the night before a race, being responsible as an assistant for one of the bikes and setting up the bike for the next event. Every rider has at least two people caring for his bike and the rider, plus many other people behind the scenes, and Ken is one of those. It's a long way from when I was riding and did everything myself. Today, what we have is like a NASCAR setup for motorcycles.

Mark, my brother, is retired and enjoying life at age 69. He has been working with his son, Tim (my nephew), on a racecar as part of a pit crew but stepped away from that this season. He spent much of the past few years driving Tim around to races.

My daughter Sami works for Game Entertainment for the Phoenix Suns, where she is part of the on-court entertainment team, which handles everything entertainment-wise that goes on the court. At 23, she is already working on her doctorate in business at Grand Canyon University. She is scheduled to receive it in early 2025. She wants to pursue sports marketing and hopes to own an NBA team someday. Sami is the type of person who is relentless when she knows what she wants and sets her sights on it. I'd like to think she inherited that from me!

My son Max is in his second year at Arizona State University, pursuing a Criminal Justice degree. He wants to be a forensic investigator for the FBI, investigating crime scenes. When he was born in April 2004, I was getting Estenson Logistics up and running, traveling a lot, and working long hours, so Traci had her hands full with a newborn and a toddler. Max and I share many similarities: he always hung out with older friends and, in sports, typically competed with older kids, as I did. Born and raised in Phoenix, he always wanted to play hockey despite the limited opportunities in the desert southwest, except for travel teams that went out of state. Years later, we helped him learn to play, and he turned out to be a great shot but had to learn to move on ice skates instead of rollerblades. We regret not giving him the chance to play earlier in life. In 9th grade, he was asked to play varsity but turned it down to play with his friends at a lower level. In 10th grade, he made the jump and played varsity for the next three years. He has been "mini-me" throughout his life, but in the last few years, he has found his own path. He is a natural athlete, good at anything he tries, and seems to have inherited some of my athletic ability.

These days, Traci is taking more time for herself, backing away from taking leadership roles in some of the philanthropic work she has been doing. With Sami pursuing her dreams and Max off at college, Traci has been freed from a schedule and realizes that together, we are starting a new chapter in life, free to travel and do other things. We are figuring out what is next for us as a couple of "empty nesters."

~~~~~

If you had told me five years ago that I would be writing about my life, I would have laughed at you. I had zero interest in doing so, but Traci and some of my friends encouraged me to do so to help others. Writing this book has been therapeutic and healing as I recounted my life and its struggles. I'm grateful I took the challenge of writing this book and laying my life bare, so to speak, for the world to read. By putting my life out there and collaborating with Dave, we've grown spiritually while looking at the struggles everyone faces and recalling the healing that had taken place. Today, I don't view myself as a religious person but as a spiritual one. "Allow me to serve others and not myself" is my daily prayer. God and His grace are the only reason I am still alive, and He is everything, my absolute best friend and someone I can always count on. I look at all my past adversity as something that has helped me get to where I am today and help others. Despite lacking a traditional religious experience, I have an uncanny spiritual relationship with the God of my understanding.

I trust that we have conveyed that there is always hope in life, regardless of your status and situation. "More will be revealed when I can handle it" is one of my favorite sayings, and it's true. Think of it as walking down a dark path with a flashlight. You can't see the end of the path, but you can see far enough to take the next step. (Psalm 119:105) God wants to heal your pain and give you an abundant life. (John 10:10) I want you to walk away from reading this book thinking, "This guy got help and hope. Maybe there's hope for me." There is hope, my friend because God has not given up on you. Turn to Him today for the help and healing you need in overcoming your life struggles.

HEALTH AND WELLNESS RESOURCES

If you or someone else is struggling with an addiction, your mental health, or have suicidal thoughts please don't give up hope. **There is help out there.** Below are some resources we've gathered to start you on your journey:

Alcohol:	www.aa.org
Overeating:	www.oa.org
Gambling:	www.gamblersanonymous.org
Narcotics Anonymous:	na.org
Sex:	saa-recovery.org
Suicide:	988
Spousal Abuse:	800-799-7233
PTSD:	866-903-3787

ABOUT THE AUTHORS

Tim Estenson's journey, "On Rails," is a story of redemption and inspiration. An alcoholic at 16, he battled through the demons of alcoholism, drugs, and self-destruction. His journey was not easy, filled with moments of despair and hopelessness. But he persevered, emerging victorious and becoming sober at the age of 18.

Tim not only literally took corners smoothly and precisely as a North Dakota flat track motorcycle racer in his youth, but his exceptional handling, agility, and risk-taking in developing his multi-million-dollar trucking and logistics business led to a life of recovery, business success, and service to others.

Rediscovering his passion for motorcycle racing, he founded Estenson Racing. This platform reignited his love for the sport and help's up-and-coming riders fulfill their dreams.

Tim's journey would not have been possible without the unwavering support of his wife, Traci, who has been his pillar of strength. They, along with their two children, live in a suburb of Phoenix, Arizona, where they are also involved with several philanthropic organizations and projects.

Dave Ficere, the owner of Ficere Writing Solutions, is deeply committed to his craft. He has written, edited, or narrated more than 25 books, with a focus on helping individuals share their stories of faith. This dedication to his work is evident in his previous role as a Christian Radio broadcaster for nearly 30 years, and his experience as a news writer and editor.

When he's not immersed in the world of writing, Dave is a fervent Los Angeles Dodgers fan. He is currently ticking off his 'bucket list' of stadiums, with recent visits to Wrigley Field and Fenway Park. Dave, along with his wife Patt, an Arizona Diamondbacks fan, and their dog Koufax (named after the legendary Dodger "Sandy"), resides in a Phoenix suburb.

www.ingramcontent.com/pod-product-compliance
Ingram Content Group UK Ltd.
Pitfield, Milton Keynes, MK11 3LW, UK
UKHW051557190426
11946UKWH00026B/129